PROMETHEUS

Tony Harrison was born in Leeds in 1937. His volumes of poetry
include *The Loiners* (winner of the Geoffrey Faber Memorial
Prize), *Continuous* and *v.* (broadcast on Channel 4 in 1987,
winning the Royal Television Society Award). Recognized as
Britain's leading theatre and film poet, Tony Harrison has written
extensively for the National Theatre, the New York Metropolitan
Opera, the BBC, Channel 4, and for unique ancient spaces in
Greece and Austria. Much of his writing for the theatre is included
in *Theatre Works 1973–85*; his more recent theatre works, *The
Trackers of Oxyrhynchus*, *Square Rounds*, *The Common Chorus* and
The Prince's Play are published by Faber and Faber. His film *Black
Daisies for the Bride* won the Prix Italia in 1994. His other film/
poems, *The Gaze of the Gorgon* (winner of the Whitbread Poetry
Award), *The Blasphemers' Banquet*, his four-part poem *Loving
Memory*, *A Maybe Day in Kazakhstan* and *The Shadow of
Hiroshima*, are published by Faber and Faber in one volume. A
selection of his poetry, including *v.*, read by the author, is
available on a Faber/Penguin audiotape.

TONY HARRISON

Prometheus

faber and faber

First published in 1998
by Faber and Faber Limited
3 Queen Square London WC1N 3AU

Photoset by Parker Typesetting Service, Leicester
Printed in England by Clays Ltd, St Ives plc

A CIP record for this book
is available from the British Library
ISBN 0-571-19753-1

2 4 6 8 10 9 7 5 3 1

A Channel 4 Film in association with the Arts Council of England.

HERMES	Michael Feast
OLD MAN/GRANDAD	Walter Sparrow
MAM (10)	Fern Smith
BOY	Jonathan Waistnidge
DAD	Steve Huison
GRANDMA	Audrey Haggerty

MINERS Dave Hill, Tim Hall, Roger Gren, Ian Clayton, Paul Knaggs, James Banks, Dave Parker, Alan Hobson, Stewart Merrill

DAUGHTERS OF OCEAN Catherine Pidd, Maureen Craven, Beverley Ashby, Sue Barker, Sandra Hookham, Clare Hookham, Jane Riley, Lesley Pickersgill, Beverley Brighton, Vicky McCallister, Linda Callear, Jean McCauley

Written and directed by	Tony Harrison
Director of Photography	Alastair Cameron
Production Designer	Jocelyn Herbert
Editor	Luke Dunkley
Composer	Richard Blackford
Production Manager	Peter Flynn
Location Manager	Joel Holmes
Executive Producer	Michael Kustow
Producer	Andrew Holmes

A Holmes Associates/Michael Kustow Production

Filmed on location in Doncaster, Knottingley, Ferrybridge, Finningley, Humberside, Grimsby, Dresden, Czech Republic, Poland, Slovakia, Hungary, Romania, Bulgaria and Greece.

FIRE & POETRY

'Fire & Poetry, two great powers
that make the so-called god's world OURS.'

Prometheus [1998]

'To make films is to be a poet'

Pier Paolo Pasolini

(i)

As a child I learned to dream awake before the coal-fire in our
living room. Staring into the fire, with its ever-changing flames,
shifting coals, falling ash, and what were called 'strangers' – skins
of soot flapping on the grate – evoked in me my first poetry. My
first meditations were induced by the domestic hearth, I have
always associated staring into flames with the freedom of poetic
meditation. It has been proposed by Gaston Bachelard that it is
from brooding before flames that early man developed his interior
life. It was also my job to light the fire, and to fetch the coal up
from the cellar. With a bucket from the dark dank cellar that had
been our shelter from German air-raids and incendiary bombs, I
brought the black coal that fuelled my dreaming. I later learned
that the Latin for hearth is *focus*. And fire is what I focus on in
Prometheus. And I remembered my Latin when, filming *Prometheus*
on the roads of Romania, I saw on a forest-fire sign the word FOC.
FIRE.

(ii)

The myth of Prometheus, who brought fire to Mankind, keeps
entering history at significant moments. One of the sources of my
film is the *Prometheus Bound* of Aeschylus (525–456 BC) Most
Greek tragedy shifts its timescale from immediate suffering to
some long-term redemption through memorial ritual or social
amelioration, or simply through the very play being performed.
The performed suffering was old, the redemption contemporary.
The appeal to futurity is not simply that 'time heals' because it
brings forgetfulness and oblivion, but because creative memory is
at work, giving the suffering new form, a form to allow the

suffering to be shared and made bearable across great gaps of time. And who continually cries out across millennia to present himself to 'later mortals' as a θεαμα (something to be looked at), especially in his final words, more than Prometheus? Who calls from a remoter past than the bound Prometheus, and yet who still manifests himself when history moves in directions where defiance and unfreedom cry for help? It is a myth because of its time-scale that encompasses many generations of mortals, which continually makes us reassess our history. It might give the disappointed Utopian a refuge from despair. And maybe these days the Socialist.

No play in the ancient repertoire works over a longer time scale than *Prometheus Bound*. Or deals with more unbroken suffering. Its span is not, as in the *Oresteia*, the ten fateful years of the Trojan War, but thirty millennia: thirty millennia of tyrannical torture, thirty millennia of defiance. And so it is not surprising that at times of the collapse of ideas that might have created liberty and equality the figure of the chained Titan, Prometheus, is remembered. Nor is it surprising that for those who dramatise history as dialectical struggle Prometheus has come to embody the tyrannically restrained champion of the downtrodden and oppressed. When men feel themselves in chains the myth of the Titan re-enters history. Out of hopelessness comes a new need for the chained martyr's undiminished hope, though every day Zeus's eagle tears the liver from his body:

> To suffer woes which Hope thinks infinite;
> To forgive wrongs darker than death or night;
> To defy Power, which seems omnipotent;
> To love and bear; to hope till Hope creates
> From his own wreck the thing it contemplates;
> Neither to change, nor falter, nor repent;
> This, like thy glory, Titan, is to be
> Good, great and joyous, beautiful and free;
> This alone Life, Joy, Empire, and Victory.

So Shelley concludes his own *Prometheus Unbound*, when the wreck that Hope had to contemplate was the failure of the French Revolution to deliver liberty, equality and fraternity. But hope is also created out of the contemplation of the wreck of tyrannies, earlier despotisms demolished over a long period of time, not overthrown by revolution, with Nature running riot over ruined imperial stones. It was precisely this spectacle that Shelley had all around him as he composed his *Prometheus Unbound* in Rome in 1819. Shelley found this everywhere in the ruins of the imperial city:

> Rome has fallen, ye see it lying
> Heaped in undistinguished ruin:
> Nature is alone undying.
> > 'Fragment: Rome And Nature'

And specifically in the Baths of Caracalla, which he chose as his alfresco study in which to write his play. These grandiose baths, built by the Emperor Caracalla (211–217) on the Aventine hill of Rome and enlarged by Elagabalus (218–222) and Alexander Severus (222–235), were in use until AD 537, when the Goths of Vitgis cut the aqueducts of Rome. The famous Farnese Hercules, the hero who finally killed the tormenting eagle of Zeus and freed Prometheus, stood in the colonnaded passage between the *frigidarium* and the *tepidarium*. The ruins of the ideals of the French Revolution turned Shelley to the myth, and the famous posthumous painting by Joseph Severn, now in the Keats-Shelley House in Rome, shows him working on his *Prometheus Unbound* in 1818/19 in the ruins of the Baths of Caracalla. Such ruins revealed to Shelley the proof that even the greatest of powers come to an end, a suitable ambience in which to compose his *Prometheus Unbound*. And the Baths of Caracalla is still an appropriate place in which to contemplate the ruins of time and the collapse of empire, with their braced brick molars, thirds of arches, seagulls on the jagged rims fenced off with hazard tape, or with a red-and-white warning hurdle. The bricks abraded back to rock and dust. Signs which give you a clue to the vast ruins: APODYTERIUM; NATATIO. The whole vast collection of fragmentary walls braced and netted, sometimes held together, by the roots of briar and blackberry laurel, yew, fig. And fennel – perhaps the most appropriate plant to preside over this preface as it was in a stalk of fennel that Prometheus hid the fire he stole for Mankind. This preface to my *Prometheus* film was sketched there, as Shelley's *Prometheus Unbound* was 180 years ago, in the Terme di Caracalla,

Rome. The whole of Shelley's great poem, which I had in my pocket, seems to end back in the Baths of Caracalla when, as Richard Holmes writes, 'the vision has dissolved and Shelley is sitting within the blossoming labyrinths of the Baths of Caracalla'. These ruins helped Shelley to give the struggle between Zeus and the chained Titan a millennial scale. Zeus or a Roman Emperor, or a regime intended for all time, could also be like Ozymandias:

> 'My name is Ozymandias, king of kings:
> Look on my works, ye Mighty, and despair!'
> Nothing beside remains. Round the decay
> Of that colossal wreck, boundless and bare,
> The lone and level sands stretch far away.
>   'Ozymandias' (1817)

It is the time that dealt, again in Shelley's words, with Bonaparte:

> A frail and bloody pomp which Time has swept
> In fragments towards Oblivion.
>   'Feelings of a Republican on the Fall of Bonaparte' (1816)

Everything toppling into the 'dust of creeds outworn' (*Prometheus Unbound*, 1.697). The 'vast and trunkless legs of stone' of the ruin of Ozymandias could well refer in 1989 to the dismantled and toppled statues of Lenin and various Eastern European Communist leaders in bronze or stone all over the Eastern bloc. Ozymandias and the ruins of the Baths of Caracalla for Shelley, as the toppled Berlin wall for us, were evidence of time overturning the tyrannies, an assurance that Prometheus would not suffer for ever.

Byron has similar reactions to Rome and the triumph of time:

> Oh Rome! my country! city of the soul!
> The orphans of the heart must turn to thee,
> Lone mother of dead empires! and control
> In their shut breasts their petty misery.
> What are our woes and sufferance? Come and see
> The cypress, hear the owl, and plod your way
> O'er steps of broken thrones and temples, Ye!
> Whose agonies are evils of a day –
> A world is at our feet as fragile as our clay.
>   *Childe Harold's Pilgrimage*, LXVIII

x

Cypress and ivy, weed and wallflower grown
Matted and mass'd together, hillocks heap'd
On what were chambers, arch crush'd, column strown
In fragments, choked up vaults, and frescos steep'd
In subterranean damps, where the owl peep'd,
Deeming it midnight: – Temples, baths or halls?
Pronounce who can; for all that Learning reap'd
From her research hath been, that these are walls –
Behold the Imperial Mount! 'tis thus the mighty falls.
    Childe Harold's Pilgrimage, CVII

Byron's statue by the Danish sculptor Thorvaldsen in the garden
of the Villa Borghese has a thoughtful poet seated on a fallen
fragment of column and beside it a human skull, imperial might
and fragile clay made one in time's momentum. The momentum
that crushed hope and Prometheus who kept it burning like a
torch of liberty. The Titan has been described as 'a primordial
figure in the history of hope'. In Shelley and Byron's time the
'history of hope' had met its obstacles, and if Prometheus was, as
he was for Shelley, 'the saviour and the strength of suffering man'
(*PU* 1.817) and the patron saint of the overthrow of tyrannical
power, then he too was tormented by that shrivelling of hope in
Man. One of the things that Prometheus is tortured by, apart from
the eagle eating his liver, is the vision sent to him of what is in fact
Shelley's own anguish, the failure of the French Revolution:

Names are there, Nature's sacred watchwords, they
Were borne aloft in bright emblazonry;
The nation thronged around, and cried aloud,
As with one voice, Truth, liberty, and love!
Suddenly fierce confusion fell from heaven
Among them: there was strife, deceit, and fear:
Tyrants rushed in, and did divide the spoil.
This was the shadow of the truth I saw.
    Prometheus Unbound, 1.648–55

Byron also writes with Shelley's bitterness about the effect of the
failed French Revolution on Europe's struggle for freedom:

But France got drunk with blood to vomit crime,
And fatal have her Saturnalia been

To Freedom's cause, in every age and clime;
Because the deadly days which we have seen,
And vile Ambition, that built up between
Man and his hopes an adamantine wall,
And the base pageant last upon the scene,
Are grown the pretext for the eternal thrall
Which nips life's tree, and dooms man's worst – his
   second fall.
   Childe Harold's Pilgrimage, XCVII

Both Byron and Shelley call on Prometheus and his
commitment to Man's future to help them weather what Shelley
calls in his Preface to *The Revolt of Islam* 'the age of despair' that,
for intellectuals like him, followed on what he had to call, in the
lines above, the 'strife, deceit and fear' of the French Revolution.
What is needed for the creation of a just, independent society after
this setback, writes Shelley, is 'resolute perseverance and
indefatigable hope, and long-suffering and long-believing
courage'. Such perseverance and indefatigable hope are
symbolically pre-eminent in the apparently hopelessly chained
Prometheus. In the Preface to *The Revolt of Islam* (1818) Shelley
writes:

> The revulsion occasioned by the atrocities of the demagogues,
> and the re-establishment of successive tyrannies in France, was
> terrible, and felt in the remotest corner of the civilised world.
> This influence has tainted the literature of the age with the
> hopelessness of the minds from which it flows. Metaphysics,
> and inquiries into moral and political science, have become little
> else than vain attempts to revive exploded superstitions, or
> sophisms like those of Mr Malthus, calculated to lull the
> oppressors of mankind into a security of everlasting triumph.

The 'oppressors of Mankind' are gathered together as 'the
Oppressor of Mankind', as Shelley called Zeus/Jove when, in the
same spirit as *The Revolt of Islam*, he wrote *Prometheus Unbound* in
the following year.

(iii)

Shelley considered *Prometheus Unbound* his finest piece of work. It sold less than a score of copies, and is still never given a theatrical presentation or even thought of as a play. H. S. Mitford is a typical example. He edited *The Oxford Book of English Romantic Verse 1798–1837* (1935), and like so many editors of dreary anthologies excluded the poetry from dramatic works, giving a very narrowed view of the range of verse. Songs from plays were admitted as they fitted the lyrical cliché. And he also made an exception of a passage from Shelley's *Prometheus Unbound* on the grounds that 'no one would call that a play'. Shelley's *play* (and indeed most of the dramatic efforts of the Romantic poets) is considered untheatrical and unplayable, and judged by the theatrical clichés of today it may seem irredeemable as a dramatic text. But George Bernard Shaw had the musical and Wagnerian insight to see in Shelley's *Prometheus Unbound* 'an English attempt at a Ring', and Wagner's ideas were deeply inspired by Aeschylus. Later critics, like Timothy Webb (1986), have also sought to justify and incorporate Shelley's attempts into the theatrical canon by stressing operatic models: '*Prometheus Unbound* in particular seems to owe a considerable debt to operatic models as well as to masque and, more obviously, to its Aeschylean prototype. Its exploration of musical analogies and its use of strategies and structures from opera and ballet extend the boundaries of dramatic form.' Isabel Quigly makes similar operatic parallels in her introduction to Shelley's selected poetry (Penguin Poetry Library): '. . . *Prometheus Unbound*, a drama on so heroic a scale that his lack of dramatic competence does not matter, for this is not theatre but huge/metaphysical grand-opera, where the scenery can creak if the singing is good enough.'

The preponderant cliché of naturalism in contemporary British theatre makes anything even a little different unwelcome, but there are salutory reminders from an Indian scholar whose traditions of non-European drama give him a sympathy for Shelley's play greater than any expressed in Shelley's native land:

It clearly represents a rejection of the literary theatre as known to the Western World. But all theatre is not the property of the relatively small continent of Europe. Shelley's thought and art in his singular iridescent poem seem in luminous fashion to look beyond the confines of Western usage and tradition to the more

imaginative dramas of other civilisations, to the theatre of the
dance, with its accompanying music, or to the theatre of the
dancing shadow puppets of the Far East. His imagination
deliberately and resoundingly defies our more temporal stages
as developed for our human actors in flesh and blood. Curiously
enough, on the contrary, it even invites Indian play of shadows,
or puppet shows based on the epics.

And H. H. Anniah Gowda, the Professor of English at the
University of Mysore, goes on to say something that confirms my
despair of most contemporary theatre and that gave me, in what
I've italicised, a nudge in the direction of my own *Prometheus*:

> It is easy to conceive Shelley's infinite choreographic work as a
> chant for a dance not as yet created, a libretto for a musical
> drama not as yet composed, a poetic companion to some *future
> revelation in the imaginative film* . . . *Prometheus Unbound* can be
> a dramatic reality only when the theatre itself is unbound from
> innumerable restrictions now confining it so firmly that this
> liberation remains for the less daring and imaginative minds an
> unthinkable change . . . The student of practicable drama at the
> present does ill to overlook even so apparently anti-theatrical a
> text as Shelley's drama-poem. In such unlikely sources may lie
> concealed the seeds of a future burgeoning. Now that the winter
> has come to the theatre, even a new *Prometheus Unbound* may
> not be far behind.
>
> (*Dramatic Poetry from Medieval to Modern Times*, Madras, 1972)

I have always thought that Shelley's *Prometheus Unbound* had
'seeds of a future burgeoning', though the snow still lies deep on
most of our stages and the footsteps poets have made on them
have disappeared under new chill flurries. I can only echo Ibsen
when, in the face of hostility to his *Peer Gynt*, he asserted that 'My
book *is* poetry; and if it isn't, it will become such.' Shelley's play,
unfortunately, is still in the process of becoming. And I have to say
that my *Prometheus is* a film; and if it isn't, it will become such!

(iv)

Shelley's reaction to the idea of writing a parallel trilogy to that of
Aeschylus, with détente finally achieved between the punisher and

the punished, was that he wanted absolutely no reconciliation. 'I was averse', Shelley writes in his Preface to *Prometheus Unbound*, 'from a catastrophe so feeble as that of reconciling the Champion with the Oppressor of mankind.' No détente. As we do not possess the other two plays of the *Prometheia*, Aeschylus' Promethean trilogy, then we are left with undiluted defiance and enduring tyranny.

Karl Marx is said to have observed that he regretted that Shelley died at the age of twenty-nine, 'for Shelley was a thorough revolutionary and would have remained in the van of socialism all his life'. Marx's disputed remark was at the expense of Byron, who Marx is said to have prophesied would have become a 'reactionary bourgeois'. Paul Foot takes up this speculation in his *Red Shelley* (1984) and imagines Byron supporting the Reform Bill of 1832, which enfranchised only property owners, and Shelley supporting the extension of the Bill and the Chartist movement. These speculations are, according to the former leader of the Labour Party, Michael Foot, extremely unfair on Byron (*The Politics of Paradise: A Vindication of Byron*, 1988). After Byron's death in Greece, Michael Foot points out that Heinrich Heine (1797–1856) actually identifies Byron with Prometheus himself: 'He defied miserable men and still more miserable gods like Prometheus.' And the same identification was made all over Europe. Adam Mickiewicz (1798–1855), Poland's national bard, wrote that Byron 'had cursed and fumed like Prometheus, the Titan, whose shade he loved to evoke so often'. And in Italy, Mazzini (1805–72), the great soul of the Risorgimento, honoured the dead poet in these words: 'never did the "eternal spirit of the chainless mind" make a brighter apparition amongst us. He seems at times a transformation of that immortal Prometheus, of whom he has written so nobly, whose cry of agony, yet of futurity, sounded above the cradle of the European world.'

After Shelley and Byron Prometheus' 'cry of agony yet futurity' gradually began to be identified with the struggle for socialism. Eight years after the death of Byron, Thomas Kibble Hervey (1799–1859) published an 83-line poem *Prometheus* (1832) which places the chained Titan, with contemporary geographical accuracy, in the frozen plains of Russia, with its oppressed serfs taking inspiration from their manacled champion:

Amid this land of frozen plains and souls
Are beating hearts that wake long weary nights,
Unseen, to listen to thy far-off sigh;
And stealthily the serf, amid his toils,
Looks up to see thy form against the sky.

He writes of kings as 'the petty Joves of earth' and has a vision of freedom and deliverance with the masses, inspired by the American example of monarchless democracy, coming to liberate Prometheus:

And thou shalt rise – the vulture and the chain
Shall both be conquered by thine own stern will!
Hark! o'er the far Atlantic comes a sound
Of falling fetters, and a wild, glad cry
Of myriad voices in a hymn to thee!
Hail to that music! To its tune sublime
Shall march the legions of the world of mind,
On to thy rescue, o'er each land and sea.

The second step towards Prometheus becoming a patron saint of socialism was probably the association of the Titan Fire-Giver with the heavy industries and technologies dependent on fire in one form or another. 'Thanks to fire . . . man has attained domination over the world,' writes Paul Ginestier in *The Poet and the Machine* (1961). In the heartland of German industry in the nineteenth century the title of the magazine that kept its readers abreast with new industrial technology seemed almost inevitable: *Prometheus: Illustrierte Wochenschrift uber die Fortschritte in Gewerbe, Industrie und Wissenschaft* (Illustrated Weekly on Developments in Trade, Industry and Science: Leipzig, 1899–1921). Prometheus becomes the patron of technology and the smokestacks of the industry of the Rhine, the Ruhr, and the North of England where I myself grew up, inhaling the sulphurous fumes of the Promethean gift. 'The Iron Kingdom where his Majesty Fire reigns', as Guy de Maupassant puts it. This identification with industry transformed Prometheus from being, in the words of Timothy Richard Wutrich, in his study on *Prometheus and Faust* (1995), '[the] primordial figure in the history of the concept of hope', to being what the Marxist Classical scholar George Thomson, making the concept of hope more specifically political, calls Prometheus in *Aeschylus and Athens* (1941): 'the patron saint of the proletariat'. Karl Marx himself, who referred to Prometheus as 'the first saint and martyr of the philosopher's calendar', was, during his editorship of the *Rhineland Gazette*, depicted in cartoons as Prometheus bound to a printing press with the Prussian eagle gnawing his liver. At his feet, like the chorus of the Oceanides, the Daughters of Ocean represented the cities of the Rhineland pleading for freedom.

When the English poet and magazine editor John Lehmann wrote a book on the Caucasus in 1937 he called it *Prometheus and the Bolsheviks* – 'because Prometheus is the oldest symbol of the Caucasus, and can at the same time be considered as the oldest symbol of what the Bolsheviks have had as their aim: the deliverance of man from tyranny and barbarism by the seizure of material power.' On a *Sovtorgflot* boat on the Black Sea, heading for Sukhum in Georgia, Lehmann has a dream of meeting Prometheus, who says to him: 'I find myself passionately on the side of the Bolsheviks when I hear accounts of the Civil War struggles. *It reminds me of my own struggles with Jove over the fire business* [my italics].' Prometheus then announces that he has made a momentous decision: 'I have decided', says Prometheus, 'to join the Party!' Then Lehmann wakes from his dream, and the boat docks in Sukhum.

But as Prometheus gathers his supporters, so does the tyrant Zeus, whose parallel manifestations take on historically terrifying forms. As Shelley wrote, Humanity is 'heaven-oppressed' (*PU*, 1.674). The ministers of Jupiter trample down the 'beloved race' of Prometheus. These ministers are 'thought-executing'. The brain of Jove is 'all-miscreative' (*PU*, 1.448). All monolithic ideologies, religious and political, are 'miscreative'. Zeus (or Jupiter, or Jove) is the image of recurrent tyranny and he wants to destroy Mankind through human agents like Hitler and Stalin; and, though Prometheus foiled his destruction of Mankind once by stealing fire, perhaps he now plays into the tyrant's hands by giving men the freedom to use fire as they will. And because Prometheus, in his socialist avatar, is the champion of the industrial worker, the miner, the steel-worker, Zeus particularly glories in fiery destruction and smoky pollution, and Mankind's slower death by poisoning the earth with factories fuelled by Promethean power.

xvii

The hasty and massive industrialisation of the socialist countries in the 1950s took little heed of the ecological consequences, and guide-books to places like Romania glorified the industrial sites in a way that suggests that they were conducting Prometheans around the sacred temples of their Titanic champion. 'The town of Bicaz is already an important tourist centre,' we read in *Romania: A Guide Book* (Bucharest, 1967). And why? 'In this region beside the hydro-power station of Stejarul we find . . . the new mines of non-ferrous metals at Lesul Ursului and of barites at Obcina Voronetului, the cement mill at Bicaz, the timber-processing factory at Vaduri, the refinery at Darmesti – all of them industrial units built by socialism in its forward march.' The prose is straining to become a Promethean poetry, and the cumulative roll-call with its chemical and geographical names could in the hands of an Aeschylus or a Milton have epic scale. The writer is always relieved to leave natural scenic surroundings for the lyrical nomenclature of the chemical industries:

> Presently, however, this charming natural scenery will have to give way to a monumental achievement of man's hand. We are nearing the big industrial aggregate of Gheorghiu Georghiu-Dej Town [with its] huge tanks, cylindrical towers, silvery pipes, black pipes, white pipes curling gracefully . . . It supplies coke for electrodes, propane propylene for phenol, and butane-butylene for synthetic rubber.

Copşa Mică, once the most polluted town in Romania and maybe the world, whose carbon-black factory that blackened everything around it – houses, hills, people, sheep – and which is now derelict and its workers jobless and hopeless, gets this Promethean puff:

> We continue to travel along the Tirnava Valley and after 10 km we reach Copşa Mică, one of the important centres of the Romanian chemical industry, nicknamed the 'retort' town. We shall be struck by the bizarre outline of the carbon-black works – looking like a dark castle – and our attention will be arrested by the installations of the sulphuric acid works and of the first Romanian works for polyvinyl chloride . . .

In my film Hermes takes the golden statue of Prometheus to have it daubed and desecrated with carbon black thrown by the redundant workers of Copşa Mică. It took the whole crew days to get clean, and for weeks carbon black soiled everything we had. When we crossed the border into Bulgaria, the border guards asked our interpreter if British people were always so dirty.

The pattern of rapid Promethean industrialisation was replicated all over the former socialist world. The steel works of Nowa Huta, where I also filmed, were hurriedly constructed on a site where there was neither iron ore nor coal to create a proletarian work force 10 kilometres east of the ancient university town of Krakow, with its longstanding traditions of culture and religion. The idea of a bright future based on industrialisation and five-year plans created vast, technically out-of-date temples to Prometheus which are now, since 1989, rapidly becoming derelict 'rustbelts' with thousands out of work. The same fate has happened to the most 'Promethean' industries in Great Britain, coal and steel. Nick Danziger in *Danziger's Britain* uses the expression 'industrial genocide' to describe this end to heroic industry, and paints a frightening picture of its aftermath of unemployment, vandalised inner cities, children without hope turning to drugs and then to crime to maintain their habit.

One of the visions sent to torment Shelley's chained Prometheus is the beginning of the Industrial Revolution and urban industrialisation:

> Look! where round the wide horizon
> Many a million-peopled city
> Vomits smoke in the bright air.
> Hark the outcry of despair.

The Prometheus of 180 years later has to harken to cries of despair from the now smokeless dereliction.

(v)

'No doubt it has often been stated that the conquest of fire definitely separated man from the animal,' writes Gaston Bachelard in *La Psychoanalyse du Feu* (1938),' but perhaps it has not been noticed that the mind in its primitive state, together with its poetry and knowledge, had been developed in meditation before a fire . . . the *dreaming man* seated before his fireplace is the man concerned with inner depths, a man in the process of

xix

development.' And Dennis Donoghue equates the theft of fire with 'the origin of consciousness': 'Fire enabled them to move from nature to culture, but it made culture a dangerous possession: *it made tragedy possible* . . . We have found the stolen fire identified with reason and knowledge, but it is probably better to identify it with the symbolic imagination . . . Above all, Prometheus made possible the imaginative enhancement of experience, the metaphorical distinction between what happens to us and what we make of the happening. That is to say, Prometheus provided men with consciousness and the transformational grammar of experience.'

The fire that primitive man gazes into and that prompts him, in his flame-lit reverie, to become a poet is one thing, the fire we are forced to gaze into as we cross millennia at the end of the twentieth century is another. The poetry from this fire-gazing is hard though essential to achieve, and is almost the artist's greatest challenge. The fire we must gaze into burns in Dresden, Hamburg, in the ovens of Auschwitz, in Hiroshima, Nagasaki, in all those places where non-combatants were burned to death; in the looted and destroyed villages of the Balkans; in the millions of Greek manuscripts and books burned in the library of Alexandria by Moslem fanatics, in Jewish and so-called 'decadent' books in Germany burned by Nazi fanatics; in the bonfire of the books of dissidents, including the poetry of Yannis Ritsos, in front of the Temple of Zeus in Athens under the Metaxas dictatorship; in Moslem books in the Institute for Oriental Studies of Sarajevo destroyed by rockets on 17 May 1992, with the incineration of the entire library of documents and manuscripts of Ottoman Bosnia; in Salman Rushdie's *Satanic Verses* burned by affronted Moslems in Yorkshire, England. The fire in which Man discovered his poetry is used to destroy poetic endeavour. Poetry will either be tempered in that burning history or disappear. The meditative hearth now contains the Holocaust and the H-bomb. 'The atom smashers may be regarded as the most Promethean of the Prometheans. By releasing the power latent in the nucleus of the atom they made the theft of Prometheus a very minor piece of effrontery.' (Robert S. De Ropp, *The New Prometheans: Creative and Destructive Forces in Modern Science*, London 1972).

The flames that created reverie create nightmares. The flames that once created man's capacity for dreaming are now fuelled by tragedies, and the expression we seek from their contemplation has to imagine those worst things in the dancing fires that cast our shadows into the next millennium. And if I say that the fire offered by the Prometheus of Aeschylus had not yet acquired the accretions of our bestial and barbaric human history, I would have to add that I think that Aeschylus gazed into what, for him in the 5th century BC, was an equivalent historical destruction, the eradication of an entire civilisation in the razing of the city of Troy. The beacons that brought the news of the fall of Troy after ten years to Argos and the torches that accompanied the procession that honours the Furies at the end of the *Oresteia*, were lit from the annihilation of Troy. The gift of fire was already ambiguous to Aeschylus. The destructive had to give birth to the celebratory fire, and the celebratory fire, like our own VJ street bonfires in 1945, can never be a different element from the destructive flame. The images of torches in procession, the destructive element as a redemptive symbol, is paralleled in the way Jewish pilgrims to Auschwitz place *Yohrzeit* (Remembrance) candles in the ovens where over a million were cremated, a candle into the heart of dark, destroying flame.

(vi)

The *Prometheus Bound* of Aeschylus ends with a great cry to the light that is common to all and that unites the audience with the surrounding universe and their suffering champion:

ω παντων
αιθηρ κοινον φαος ειλισσων,
εσορας μ' ως εκδικα πασχω
(vv.1125–7)

This common light is at the heart of the experience of Greek Tragedy, as I have written in my introduction to my play *The Trackers of Oxyrhynchus* (Faber, 1990). Why, you might ask, should I – who have often claimed that we cannot understand the essence of ancient tragedy unless we remember that the common light united audience and performer, and have refused all offers to have my theatrical presentations filmed – use the cinema for my *Prometheus*?

xxi

In fact, many years ago, I had wanted to stage the original play of Aeschylus in Yorkshire, as one of what have been called my *kamikaze* performances, on a Caucasus of coalslack on some colliery spoil heap close to a power station. It became a cinema venture because of a feeling I had that my poetic reveries in front of our living room coal-fire and my earliest experiences of films were connected. Wolfgang Schivelbusch, a German historian of the industrialisation of light in the nineteenth century, articulates a parallel that I had always felt – between gazing into fire where our poetry began, and looking at images in the cinema, which needs the surrounding darkness:

> In light-based media, light does not simply illuminate existing scenes, it creates them. The world of the diorama and the cinema is an illusory dream world that light opens up to the viewer . . . He can lose himself in it in the same way that he can submerge himself in contemplating the campfire or a candle. In this respect the film is closer to the fire than the theatre. An open-air performance in bright daylight is quite feasible, while a camp-fire in the light of day is as senseless, even invisible, as a film projected in daylight. The power of artificial light to create its own reality only reveals itself in darkness. In the dark, light is life.

The connection between my obsession with fire and my obsession with movies led me to make a film about fire and poetry. The other factor which led me to the cinema is the way the size of the cinema screen can give heroic stature to the most humble of faces, and this became an essential requirement in a film where the most unlikely wheezing ex-miner is slowly made to represent Prometheus himself. Men projected onto large screens could become Titans or gods.

In 1978 I worked at the Metropolitan Opera in New York with John Dexter, doing a new English libretto for Smetana's opera *Prodana Nevesta* (The Bartered Bride). The designer was the great Czech scenographer Josef Svoboda, with whom I spent time in Prague as I was researching my scenario in Bohemia. He gave me a book on his work by Jarka Burian, *The Scenography of Josef Svoboda* (Wesleyan University Press, 1971). I had lived and worked in Prague in the sixties and had seen many of his truly innovative designs in the theatres there and his thrilling combinations of film and stage at the *Laterna Magika*, so I was very glad to have a book which documented these productions and gave me detailed information on those I hadn't seen. One in particular stayed in my mind: the Staatsoper, Munich, production by Everding of Carl Orff's opera *Prometheus* in 1968. Svoboda tried to solve the problem of a man projecting a Titan by using simultaneous video to literally *project* the singing Prometheus onto the rock where he was bound so that the tenor sang from between his own projected Titan's eyes. Svoboda described his ingenious solution thus:

> . . . the main device was the use of live television to project an enlarged image of Prometheus' face onto the very surface of the rock to which he was nailed, in other words, we saw Prometheus 'in' the image of his face, thereby providing tremendous emphasis to his torment. We used the technique at special moments only, for maximum impact. The ending, during which I used dozens of low-voltage units, had its own special effectiveness. I had the entire frame of the proscenium lined with low-voltage units aimed at the rock and Prometheus. During the ending of the opera, the intensity of these units was gradually increased at the same time that the rock was gradually being withdrawn. The intensity of the special lights increased to a painful, blinding glare in which the TV image faded and the rock began to function as a mirror. The audience was blinded for nearly a full minute, in the meantime the whole setting – the rock and the stairs – disappeared, leaving only a blank space. Prometheus was consumed in the fire of light.

(vii)

What remained to do was to put the poetry I had nurtured in the flames of the family hearth into the cinema. I happen to believe that film and poetry have a great deal in common. One of the first things I learned from the ten film/poems I have made was that poetry could enter the inner world of people in documentary situations. Auden, probably the first poet to write verse specifically for a screen documentary, *Nightmail* (1936), is reported to have said in a lecture on 'Poetry and Film': 'Poetry can also be used to express the thoughts of characters, in rather the same way as

Eugene O'Neill introduces "the interior voice" in *Strange Interlude*.' (Auden's lecture in 1936 to the North London Film Society is included in the form of an authorised report as an appendix in Edward Mendelson's edition of Auden's *Plays and Other Dramatic Writings*, Faber, 1989).

I disagree wholeheartedly with Auden's opinion that 'The generally accepted metrical forms cannot be used in films, owing to the difficulty of cutting the film exactly according to the beat without distorting the visual content.' In my own film/poems I have used the quatrain of Gray's *Elegy* and the quatrain of Fitzgerald's *Rubaiyat of Omar Khayyam*, as well as octosyllabic couplets. Auden's remark, of course, only applies to the kind of task Auden was set – that is, to compose verse to an already edited picture, as a film composer usually produces his score. Although I sometimes work in this way, when the editor has come up with an exciting sequence, I usually begin drafting even before the editor has done his first rough assembly. In fact, when I wasn't on the shoot itself (and after my first collaboration with the BBC director Peter Symes, I always was present and sometimes composing on the spot), I would see all the rushes and begin sketching lines and sequences.

The person who wrote notes on Auden's lecture observes that 'Mr Auden even found it necessary to time his spoken verse with a stop-watch in order to fit it exactly to the shot on which it commented.' Auden was working before the video machine made it possible to have frame-accurate time code and easily re-played sequences. And perhaps the new digital editing has made it possible to experiment much more with the relations between poetry and film. Whereas manual editing on the Steenbeck gives a run-up, albeit in fast forward, to the sequence being worked on, and therefore a quick reprise of the wider context, digital editing with its speed can allow you to try many different variations in much shorter time. It also allows the editor to call up clusters of related imagery from any part of the logged and telecined rushes. This can be the visual equivalent of laterally garnered clusters of poetic imagery, and my deep-rooted way of letting disparate images grow together has been fed by the Avid or Lightwords editing programmes.

Auden clearly wanted to learn more about the technicalities of film-making in the thirties and to explore the possibilities of what he could do, not after the film was edited, but before and even during the shooting. He was to have been co-director on Grierson's planned sequel to *Nightmail* to be called *Air Mail to Australia*. The endeavour was abandoned, but it shows that Auden was keen to extend his relationship with film. In 1935 Auden served as production manager and assistant director on another GPO Film Unit production, *Calendar of the Year*, in which he also played a small role as Father Christmas! Auden clearly saw the possibilities of film and poetry and seems to have been willing to apprentice himself to all the processes, with a view to doing what I, in fact, have ended up doing in my own film/poems – being there as a constant presence during the shoot with a very sympathetic colleague like Peter Symes, and then, following the logic of the organic process developed during our collaborations, directing the films myself.

Another great figure in British cinema, the documentary film-maker Humphrey Jennings, was also a poet both on the page and in his cinematic practice, and the perception of the affinity could also be found at the same time in the Soviet Union. Sergei Eisenstein began work on *Alexander Nevsky* in 1937, the year of my birth. When, he began his shooting script he was inspired by Milton's *Paradise Lost*. Thus, 'Milton's imagery of the Battle of Heaven became the battle on the ice in *Alexander Nevsky*,' writes Marie Seaton (1978), Eisenstein's biographer. He broke lines of Milton down into scenes 'to illustrate how *cinematic construction could be found in poetry.*'

Pier Paolo Pasolini was a poet before he was a film director. Even towards the end of his career a film like *Teorema* (1968) began life in the form of a verse tragedy, and Pasolini used his own verse, as Eisenstein used Milton's, as a template for cinematic construction. Victor Erice, the Spanish director of *The Spirit of the Beehive* and *The Quince Tree Sun*, said, in an interview in the *Guardian* on 1 April 1993:

> As Pasolini used to say, there is the cinema of prose and the cinema of poetry, and I try for the latter kind . . . Nowadays, prose is triumphant. We are very frightened of poetry. Hollywood deals with prose and it is as powerful in Spain as

everywhere else. I can't compete with it, still less beat it. All I would say is that there is another cinema and surely it should be allowed to exist.

There were earlier attempts before Pasolini to distinguish the cinema of prose from the cinema of poetry, and probably the first was by the Russian Victor Shklovsky, whose 'Poetry and Prose in the Cinema' was published in 1927. Maria Turovskaya, in her study of Tarkovsky, quotes Shklovsky's distinction:

> There is a cinema of prose and a cinema of poetry, two different genres; they differ not in their rhythm – or rather not only in their rhythm – but in the fact that in the cinema of poetry elements of form prevail over elements of meaning and it is they, rather than the meaning, which determine the composition.

She then goes on to ask a very important question: 'Why is it that at some moments in history the cinema feels the need for a poetic treatment of its raw material?' She answers her question by saying that this need 'is particularly sharply felt during periods of historical change, when our "normal", accepted notions and perceptions become inadequate in the face of changing realities, and new perceptions have to be developed.' And in these changing realities the often forgotten captive champion, Prometheus, tends to be remembered. Of course, she includes the films of Tarkovsky as 'poetic,' and though Tarkovsky himself grew irritated with the label, he admires and quotes his father's poetry in his films and in his 'Reflections on Cinema', *Sculpting in Time*, and himself applies the adjective to the cinema of Kurosawa. Tarkovsky, who confesses that his favourite art form is the three-line Japanese *haiku*, writes: 'I find poetic links, the logic of poetry in cinema, extraordinarily pleasing.' And among those he designates as creating 'great spiritual treasures and that special beauty which is subject only to poetry' he includes not only poets in the literary sense – Pushkin, Mandelstam and Pasternak – but also film-makers: Chaplin, the Russian Dovzhenko and the Japanese director Mizoguchi.

Pasolini also includes Chaplin and Mizoguchi, along with Bergman, as producers of 'great cinematic poems', but goes on to say that their films were not constructed according to the laws of what he calls 'the language of the cinema of poetry': 'This means that these films were not poetry, but narratives. Classic cinema was and is narrative, its language is that of prose. Its poetry is an inner poetry, as, for example, in the narratives of Chekhov or Melville.' For Pasolini the cinema of poetry means, among other things, making the spectator aware of the camera's presence, and 'a primarily formalist world-view of the author'. He speaks (in an article which, considering it is by a poet, is surprisingly bogged down with semiotic jargon) of an emergent 'prosody'.

Though much if this thinking comes from directors who are either poets themselves or have a close affinity with poetry, they are usually referring to a kind of cinema in which, as Pasolini defines it, we are aware of the camera and its movement and what he calls a 'free indirect subjective'. We are not talking about the actual use of verse, though again Tarkovsky uses his father's poetry to wonderful effect in *Mirror*. Nor are they talking about films which are cinematic versions of theatre – Shakespeare, say, or Rostand's *Cyrano* with Gerard Depardieu. My own *Prometheus* brings together my experience of film verse and theatre verse together.

There is an underlying connection between verse, metrical poetry and film which my colleague Peter Symes draws attention to in his introduction to a volume of my film/poems, *The Shadow of Hiroshima* (Faber, 1995). The 24 (or 25) frames per second have what can be called a prosodic motion. In my first experiences of the cutting room of Jess Palmer at the BBC in 1981 I realised that my own rhythmic preoccupations had a parallel in what I now think of as the scansions of edited sequences. It is not merely the 24 frames per second, nor the metrical beats in a verse line, but how they succeed one another and build into gratifications or disappointments of expectation. Maya Turovskaya describes a similar recognition with regard to Tarkovsky: 'Feeling the rhythmicity of a shot is rather like feeling a truthful word in literature.' In poetry, of course, the truthful word is also the right metrical word, the word with its truth and its sound placed on the most telling grid of the metric. The cinematic construction in poetry that Eisenstein found in Milton is paralleled by the poetic construction of cinema. And, I have always thought, the two prosodies can be plaited, metrical beat and cinematic scansion.

At the very end of the film, when there is a kind of
Gotterdammerung caused by the Old Man's flung cigarette,
intended to destroy Hermes, the golden statue of Prometheus is
consumed 'in his own concoction bloody flames'. We see real red
and yellow flames consuming the black-and-white projected
flames on the Palace Cinema screen, as the whole collected cast of
statues melt and scream like humans in a conflagration. We only
had one chance to film it, and although the charred limbs fell apart
and tumbled down the rocks in a quarry belonging to Titan
Cement, Elefsina, nonetheless what remained was the chained but
still defiantly clenched fist of the champion of Mankind, burned
off at the shoulder. And what remained of the silver statue of
Hermes was a fist still grasping his *caduceus*, the symbol of his
office. No détente!

There are times in all art when you accept what you are given,
and this was one. However, as I often do, when everyone else had
left for England I went back and looked round the quarry. At the
foot of the towering rock was the charred head of Prometheus,
matted blackened fibreglass still with the Titan's features, looking
uncannily like the photograph of the Iraqi soldier burned in his
truck on the road to Basra during the Gulf War, about whom I
had written my poem 'A Cold Coming'. What was remarkable
about this incinerated head was that in its eyes it retained the gold
leaf it had been painstakingly gilded with. So that for all its having
passed through holocaust it retained its golden visions. The vision
seen by the golden eyes in the carbonised profile isn't diminished.
They take their sheen and glitter from 'the fire of light', from the
future, from the flicker of the screen whenever their journey is
projected, and witnessed by new eyes. As I held the head I
remembered that wonderful poem of Yannis Ritsos on the
Bulgarian poet Geo Melev (1895–1925), who had a glass eye, and
when he was arrested and burned alive by the police, all that was
left of him in the crematorium was the blue glass eye:

> His eye is being kept in the Museum of Revolution
> like a seeing stone of the struggle. I saw his eye.
> In his pupil there was the full story of the Revolution,
> blue scenes of blood-stained years

blue scenes with red flags
with dead who carry in their raised hands a blue day.
His eye never closes,
this eye keeps vigil over Sofia.
This eye is a blue star in all the nights.
This eye sees and illuminates and judges.
Whoever looks at this eye wins back his eyes.
Whoever looks at this eye sees the world.
   (trans. Ninetta Makrinikola)

Poetry rises out of its own ashes and continues its ancient dream
in front of fire. Not only the animated flame but also smoking ash
and cinders with their bits of bone, rings, a blue glass eye, the
golden pupils of the first champion of Mankind, strike the
aboriginal poetic spark. Whoever looks into the golden eyes of
Prometheus set in the cremated sockets sees the early hope of the
world and knows its late despair.

Tony Harrison   Terme di Caracalla Rome
                                 Delphi, Greece
                                 1998

Prometheus

1. EXT. COOLING TOWERS, YORKSHIRE, DAWN
The sun rises between steaming cooling towers in Yorkshire.

2. EXT. KRATOS AND BIA HEADQUARTERS, COOLING TOWER, DAY
CU of flame logo (derived from the Greek forest fire-hazard warning sign) on brilliant white door. The logo is a combination of notices forbidding activities, like NO SMOKING, *but also in its black, white and red rather reminiscent of Nazi insignia.*

  Pull back to show that the logo is on a white door at the top of staircase, with red iron railings, leading from the large cooling tower of a power station.

3. INT. CAB OF CATTLE-TRUCK, DAY
CU of black rubber glove violently hitting the horn on the steering wheel of a truck.

  Pull back to reveal: BIA (VIOLENCE) *in white overalls, black chemical exposure mask and red hard hat, sounds the horn of a cattle-truck.*

4. INT. COOLING TOWER, DAY
With the sound still blaring, cut to interior of the cooling tower. In the centre of a white circular platform with a central white and red walkway stands KRATOS (FORCE), *his head raised towards the open circle of the top of the tower as if receiving his morning briefing from Zeus. There is steam seeping through the slats on either side.*

  The 'briefing' comes from the disembodied voice of HERMES *reverberating through the cooling tower.*

VOICE OF HERMES
  Zeus commands you don the gear
  of Kratos (Force) and Violence (Bia)
  and, in this guise, you give some grief
  to those who love the fire-thief.

The blaring of the truck horn is echoed and reverberated inside the vast cooling tower.

  KRATOS *begins to walk forward towards the door of the cooling tower.*

3

KRATOS (FORCE) *has the same white overalls, black chemical exposure mask and red hard hat as* BIA (VIOLENCE).
The echoing klaxon continues abrasively and more insistently.

5. EXT. KRATOS AND BIA HEADQUARTERS, DAY
KRATOS (FORCE) *walks down the steps of the cooling tower, opens the truck door, and his black-gloved hand grasps the wrist of* BIA (VIOLENCE) *and stops the strident klaxon fanfare.*

6. INT. KRATOS AND BIA CATTLE-TRUCK, DAY
A rubber-gloved hand thrusts a tape into the cab tape deck.
String quartet music issues from cab. It is music designed to keep BIA (VIOLENCE) *tranquillized during his journey.*
BIA (VIOLENCE) *gives a final defiant blast of the horn.*
Yesterday's copy of the Doncaster Star *rests on the dashboard. It reads: 'Last Yorkshire Pit to Close Tomorrow.'*

7. EXT. COOLING TOWERS, DAY
Cattle-truck pulls away from the steaming cooling tower, which wheezes like a giant version of a smoker's lungs, the lungs of the OLD MAN.

4

8. INT. OLD MAN'S HOUSE, DAWN

OLD MAN, *up early with his cough, sees a strange truck pass through a deserted street. It is the cattle-truck driven by* FORCE *and* VIOLENCE.

OLD MAN *sits down. He picks up a paper, the same* Doncaster Star *that we saw in the passing cattle-truck and which we will see the* BOY *using to make 'chips' to light a fire. The paper announces the closure of the last pit in Yorkshire, with a picture of Michael Heseltine, in an article reviewing the whole struggle over pit closures from the Miners' Strike of 1984 to the present.*

OLD MAN *gobs at the picture of Heseltine and the coaly green phlegm runs down the picture.*

OLD MAN (*looking at paper*)
    Bastard Heseltine!

He screws up the paper with the phlegm and throws it into the dead coal-fire grate behind the one-bar electric fire.

OLD MAN
    Bastard coal!

OLD MAN *stares at his carving of 'Striking Miner, 1984' in the Promethean pose. It is a carving in coal of a miner with a defiantly raised right fist. Cattle-truck string-quartet music leading to:*

9. INT. PARENTS' BEDROOM, BOY'S HOUSE, DAWN

DAD *is up and draws the curtains and sees the cattle-truck pass. He sees the Zeus painted on the roof.*

    The cattle-truck's horn is sounded violently.

    MAM *seems to be waking from a violent nightmare.*

    DAD *opens bedroom door, shouting to* BOY, *banging on his bedroom door.*

DAD
    Come on, lad, look sharp. Get t'fire going.
BOY (*from inside his room*)
    It's too hot for a fire!
DAD (*going into bathroom*)
    I want a *coal* fire burning in this house today of all days. And
    use paper not wood. And tha can stick that kettle on, while tha's
    at it.

BOY *emerges from bedroom, putting on a red Barnsley FC jersey. He goes downstairs.*

10. EXT. KIRKBY MAIN COLLIERY, SPOIL HEAP
Cattle-truck stops outside the colliery, gleaming white on the top of a black spoil heap of slack.

KRATOS *and* BIA *have a view of the colliery's winding gear. They are waiting for something to happen.*

11. INT. CAB OF CATTLE-TRUCK, DAY
KRATOS (FORCE) *opens the newspaper with the headline reading: 'Last Yorkshire Pit to Close Tomorrow'. Sub-headline: 'Arthur's Nightmare Prophecy Fulfilled'.*

The cab of the truck has, hanging from the roof, like a typical truck-driver's talisman, a little miniature Prometheus, swinging and dangling from a little chain. We see Prometheus swaying from FORCE *and* VIOLENCE*'s POV as the truck comes to a halt on top of the spoil-heap of slack.*

KRATOS (FORCE) *opens the paper, which fills the whole frame. Then he folds it up and puts it down on the ledge above the dashboard.*

Paper becomes the paper in the BOY*'s hand.*

12. INT. FRONT ROOM OF HOUSE NEAR COLLIERY, DAY/DAWN
CU on front page of newspaper announcing pit closures, the same front page we have already seen. The sound of paper being rolled, then a pair of hands rolling the page into a tube which is then flattened. BOY *is lighting the household fire by first plaiting pages from the newspapers into 'chips'. As he plaits, the* BOY *is heard reciting the homework he has to learn for class today:*

BOY
'Men had eyes but didn't see.
The sight they now have came from me.
They had ears, but never heard
the beauty of a sound or word,
so that Man's earthly life did seem,
until my deed, a cloudy dream,
until I opened ears and eyes
to all the life of earth and skies.
Before I came men would be found
in sunless dwellings underground.

They saw no difference between
the winter and the springtime scene.
Without me Man would not now know
the earth and all that lies below,
underground treasures for his use
to free him from the grip of Zeus.
With Prometheus life began
to flourish for benighted Man.
My gift of fire made Mankind free
but I stay in captivity.'

The BOY *plaits more pages, from what is in fact his Dad's archive on
the pit closures, with prominent front pages from:* Doncaster Star,
Tuesday, 13 October 1992; Yorkshire Post, *Wednesday, 14 October
1992; and various other papers saved over the years for the scrapbook of
the miners' struggle and successive pit closures.*

*He puts the 'chips' on top of some screwed-up newspaper in the fire-
grate.*

13. EXT. STREET OUTSIDE BOY'S HOUSE, DAY
Long street with BRASS BAND, *a straggling remnant of a once great
tradition, promenading and playing out the last shift of the closing
colliery.* MINER *comes out of house and joins the straggling march. We
pick them up from the front in wide and cut back to:*

14. INT. BOY'S HOUSE, DAY
BOY *puts first lumps of coal on top of his plaited paper chips and the
scrumpled paper.*

XCU of match flame. Hold on flame. BOY *looks at the match flame,
totally fascinated by it, until his fingers are burnt and he throws away
the match, then he lights another and applies the flame to the paper
quickly and throws the match into the grate.*

The fire begins in the papers and builds. To help it along the BOY
*puts a shovel over the grate and then a newspaper. The fire roars behind
headlines of Heseltine's closures of the pit.*

XCU of photo of a group of MINERS *(the twelve whose fate we will
follow) has flames dancing and roaring behind it as the fire draws, then
it browns, then bursts into flame.*

The BOY, *used to the routine, scrumples up the burning paper and
extinguishes the flames and throws the ball of paper into the fire. He*

7

burns his hand a little as he does so, and blows on the burn to cool it.

CU of fire now burning brightly. Sound of BOY blowing on burned hand blends with Brass Band music outside in the street coming nearer.

16. EXT. STREET, DAY
KIRKBY MAIN COLLIERY BAND *marches down the street, collecting* MINERS *on the last shift of the last Yorkshire pit to march to the colliery.*

17. EXT. STREET, DAY
BRASS BAND *still promenading down the street, playing the* MINERS *out of their houses.*

BRASS BAND *passes* WOMEN *waiting for works bus, 'Oceanus', to collect them for work. Badinage between the two groups.*

Oceanus bus picks up WOMEN.

18. INT. OCEANUS BUS, DAY
Badinage with driver, group badinage.

As Oceanus bus overtakes the Band, WOMEN *rush to back seat of bus, and as the band plays a crescendo they all hit the same high note in unison.*

19. EXT. STREET, DAY
We see the WOMEN *in the back window of the bus, all with mouths open, singing to a crescendo note from the Brass Band.*

Mix through to illustration in Boy's book. It shows Prometheus as a golden statue with his right fist raised in defiance and flame in a rod of fennel stalk in his left.

20. INT. BOY'S HOUSE, DAY
BOY *is still reading his Prometheus book by the fire, at a different page.*

BOY

'My gift of fire made Mankind free
but I stay in captivity.'

He turns his head at the sound of the door opening. His POV of his DAD *entering ready for the pit's last shift.* DAD *gives a small nod and smiles but grimly. He's preoccupied with this being his last day of work.*

BOY *desperately still trying to commit to memory the passage from Prometheus.*

DAD

    I don't know, lad, all that there bleeding sitting on thi backside, bloody reading.

BOY

    'ave gotta learn it for us 'omework,
    'ave *gotta* learn it!

DAD

    God knows why they feed yer all that crap.

BOY

    Ah've gotta learn this speech for t'class today.
    Bloody great chunk to learn by heart.

DAD *takes the book to have a look at it. Flicks through the pages.*

DAD (*looking at cover of book*)

    So who's Pro-me-the-us when he's at home.

BOY

    It's pronounced Pro-me-theus.
    PRO-ME-THEUS . . . USE . . . USE.

DAD

    So what bloody *use* wor 'e then?

BOY

    Well, for a start your job'd never've existed.

DAD (*gazing into the coal fire*)

    It dun't no more!

BOY

    He stole fire from t'gods and gave it to men down here. So now there's coal and all that. He ended up chained to a rock for thirty thousand years, and a bloody great eagle came and ate his liver every day, as a punishment for stealing fire.

DAD

    Serves him bloody reet for thieving. And he shouldn't have bloody bothered, if pits was his idea!

DAD *notices that the papers he was saving have been burned.*

DAD

    Hey, have you burned t' papers from that lot? Ah'll clip thi lug if tha's used them papers that were there to make chips. They went reet back to '84, before tha were even born, them did, and tha's bloody burned 'em. There were photos of all t'lads in it.

Me an' all. Ah don't supposed that bothered thee a bit. Didn't you ever stop to think? I wor off to mek a scrapbook, scrap-heap book more like! It's bad enough being jobless wi'out being chucked on t'fire by thee!

DAD *picks up the Old Man's carving in coal and flings that in the fire. The carving is of a miner in pit gear in the Promethean pose and has an etched brass caption reading: 'Striking Miner, 1984'.*

DAD

Yer might as well burn your grandad's carving. It's only bloody coal.

The carving begins to burn in the fire. The brass plaque saying 'Striking Miner, 1984' melts in the flame.
DAD *grabs the book the* BOY *is reading.*

DAD

I'll chuck this bloody book of thine in t'fire! Your bloody what's his bloody name 's off into his own concoction, bloody flames. Serves 'im reet for thieving, and serves thee reet for taking no bloody notice.
BOY (*struggling to retrieve his book.*)
It belongs to t' school. They'll mek us pay.
And after today there won't be that much brass.
DAD
I'll give thi bloody brass.
I'll show bloody Goldenballs what for!

DAD *snatches book. He rips pages out of it and flings them into the fire.*

DAD

Yer bloody fire-giver's gone up t'flue.

DAD *storms out of the room back into the kitchen, slamming the door.*
   BOY *manages to retrieve a page of the book with the charred fragment of the golden* STATUE OF PROMETHEUS *on it. He clenches it in his fist, still smoking, and shouts angrily at the kitchen door.*

BOY

Burning books 's what Nazis do.

DAD *comes racing back out of the kitchen and clips the* BOY *round the head. The* BOY *runs out of the house. His foot kicks a toy fire-engine as he runs.*

20. EXT. SAME HOUSE, DAY
BOY *opens the door and runs out, holding his head and sobbing, just as the Brass Band come to play his Dad out. When the* BOY *sees his* DAD *he begins to run away down the street, and camera moves in to CU of* DAD *looking hurt and puzzled and up then to show* MAM (10) *leaning out of the bedroom window.*

MAM
    Jack, come back. He didn't mean it. He's upset,
    your Dad.

21. EXT. STREET, DAY
Cut to BOY *running with Brass Band in background behind.*

BOY
      Nazi get!

22. EXT. BOY'S HOUSE, DAY
MAM'*s face registers that she's had no response. She leans further out of*

the window and then with a sigh retreats. As she pulls back into the room, and her eyes make an upward movement of despair and resignation, camera follows the eye-movement and cranes up beyond her to the smoking chimney of the house and following the direction of the smoke reveals the steaming cooling towers of the power station.
    Cut to:

23. EXT. COOLING TOWERS, DAY
CU of shadows of steam crossing the bodies of the cooling towers left to right.

24. EXT. KIRKBY MAIN COLLIERY, SPOIL HEAP, DAY
Cooling towers in background. BOY *runs over the pit-hill en route to the wrecked bus yard.*

25. EXT. STREET, DAY
MAM *hurries down street after the runaway* BOY. *She passes* BRASS BAND, *who have just played her husband out of his house.*

26. INT. OLD MAN'S HOUSE, DAY
CU of the glowing single element in a one-bar electric fire. In the curved silver surface divided by the element is the reflection of the OLD MAN. *He is wheezing heavily.*
    On his mantelpiece are carvings of miners done in coal. There is one identical to the 'Striking Miner, 1984' in the Promethean pose that DAD *threw in the fire.*
    OLD MAN *tears a strip of paper from same* Doncaster Star *we saw the* BOY *use to light the fire. He twists the paper and lights it at the electric element, then lights a cigarette.*
    CU of OLD MAN's *reflection in electric fire as he lights his fag.*
    The first drag gives him a terrible coughing fit. He drops the lighted spill onto the carpet and stamps out the fire with his slipper. Frantically tries to sweep up the blackened paper and clean the black mark on the carpet.

27. INT. UPSTAIRS, OLD MAN'S HOUSE, DAY
GRANDMA, *the wife of the* OLD MAN, *is looking through the bedroom net curtains at the marching Band. She's in her nightie and there are tears flowing down her cheeks.*
    She sniffs the air, smells the OLD MAN's *cigarette smoke and hears the coughing fit. She turns and shouts:*

GRANDMA
    Are you lighting up again, you barmy beggar? You'll be

underground again sooner than you think. And if you're going
to be carving damned coal all day put some papers down.

28. INT. OLD MAN'S HOUSE, DOWNSTAIRS, DAY
OLD MAN *makes a 'stop nagging' face. Then is racked by coughing.*
   *CU on coughing mouth, then cut to Brass Band, which seems to
'translate' the coughing into staccato brass.*
   OLD MAN *puts on his overcoat and leaves the house by the back door.*

29. EXT. OLD MAN'S HOUSE, DAY
OLD MAN *comes out of the back door beneath the cooling tower.*

30. EXT. OLD MAN'S HOUSE, DAY
GRANDMA *watches the* BAND *and miners passing her house from the
bedroom window.*

31. EXT. STREET, DAY
BRASS BAND *is marching and playing at the end of the road.*
   OLD MAN *tries to catch up with the* BRASS BAND. *He coughs. He
makes another step forward.*
   *Cooling towers appear at the end of the road. They wheeze like a
smoker's lungs.*

NICK WALL

13

32. EXT. KIRKBY MAIN COLLIERY, SPOIL HEAP, DAY

A silver Statue of HERMES *pointing his caduceus (a rod with an emblem at the end depicting the same 'fire forbidden' sign we saw on the cattle-truck).*

HERMES *is pointing at* BOY *running across the vast black spoil heap in his red Barnsley FC football jersey.*

Back to HERMES *pointing from a colliery gantry at* BOY *running on the vast colliery spoil heap, a Caucasus of coal-slack alongside a conveyor pouring out coal.*

Pan from BOY *to pouring conveyor, then to:*

33. EXT. CANAL, DAY

CU of coal pouring into a coal barge.

Barge moves on canal towards cooling towers.

Heavy traffic hurtles across the A1 road-bridge over the canal.

34. EXT. PEDESTRIAN CANAL BRIDGE, DAY

OLD MAN *walks over the canal bridge dominated by the cooling towers. He leans on the parapet and coughs. In spite of the coughing fit he takes another deep drag on his fag. He smokes. He sees:*

35. EXT. CANAL PATH AND CANAL, COOLING TOWERS, DAY

MAM *runs on the canal path in the direction of the cooling towers.*

The barge we've seen filled with newly hewn coal moves, low in the water, laden with coal, towards the cooling towers of the power station.

Traffic hurtles by on the bridge above.

VOICE OF OLD MAN

I know where he'll be.

36. EXT. COOLING TOWERS, DAY

CU shadows of steam crossing the barrel chambers of the towers.

37. EXT. BUS WRECKING YARD BENEATH COOLING TOWERS, DAY

Pan down from cooling towers to discover BOY *entering bus wrecking yard. Track with* BOY *along the rusty hubs, broken windows, and doors of various buses.*

BOY *wanders round wrecked buses, into the cabs, trying seats, upstairs and downstairs. Details of dereliction. He climbs the stairs of one bus and sits down on a seat.*

BOY *looks at the charred fragment of the burned book, the golden head of Prometheus haloed in black fire-charred edges.*

NICK WALL

As he looks at the picture we hear the COLLIERY BAND *playing a mournful elegiac tune for the last shift of the last Yorkshire pit.*

38. EXT. KIRKBY MAIN COLLIERY ENTRANCE, DAY
The colliery BAND *plays the last shift into the colliery gate. Their feet crunch on the coal slack as they file in.*

39. INT. COLLIERY ENTRANCE, DAY
CU on man's hand counting out twelve piles of two brass tallies given to each MINER *as he clocks on.*

40. INT. OCEANUS BUS, DAY
WOMEN *fish factory workers chat on their bus, as the Oceanus bus passes the cooling towers.*

41. EXT. KIRKBY MAIN COLLIERY ENTRANCE, DAY
The feet of the last shift MINERS *crunch on the coal slack as they enter to the music of the colliery band.*

42. EXT. KIRKBY MAIN SPOIL HEAP, DAY
MAM *runs anxiously on top of the spoil heap with cooling towers breathing steam behind her.*

15

43. EXT. KIRKBY MAIN COLLIERY, DAY
The Band continues to play its 'threnody'. The colliery sign is reflected in the tuba bell.
CUs of various instrumentalists.

44. EXT. OCEANUS FISH FACTORY, DAY
Oceanus bus arrives at the factory.

45. EXT. BUS WRECKING YARD, DAY
BOY *leaves the upstairs of one wrecked bus past a mirror and a no-smoking sign.*

46. INT. KIRKBY MAIN COLLIERY ENTRANCE, DAY
Man's hand continues to sort the brass tallies into pairs. MINERS *clock on and take brass tallies.*

47. EXT. OCEANUS FISH FACTORY, DAY
WOMEN *enter the Oceanus fish factory.*

48. INT. KIRKBY MAIN COLLIERY, DAY
MINERS *clock on and take a pair of brass tallies from the office counter ledge.*

49. EXT. NEAR CANAL, DAY
OLD MAN *walks and wheezes past a wrecked barge dominated by cooling towers.*

50. EXT. BUS WRECKING YARD, DAY
BOY *enters the cab of another wrecked bus and starts to 'drive' it.*

51. INT. OCEANUS FISH FACTORY, DAY
Oceanus WOMEN, *now in their fish factory overalls and caps, pass through a hanging blue plastic curtain, followed by* HERMES *in the guise of an Oceanus foreman. He looks at them ominously.*

52. INT. CHANGING ROOMS, KIRKBY MAIN COLLIERY, DAY
MINERS, *now in their pit gear, pass chatting through a grimy plastic curtain.*

53. INT. CORRIDOR, KIRKBY MAIN COLLIERY, DAY
The last shift passes windows in silhouette. One of the windows is broken, showing a green tree outside. The miners' boots clatter and echo.

54. EXT. BUS WRECKING YARD, DAY

OLD MAN *enters the bus wrecking yard. He appears at the entrance of the bus the* BOY *is 'driving'.*

OLD MAN

Thi' mam's after thee!

BOY

That's just too bad.

'Cos I'm off. I got clouted by mi dad.

OLD MAN

What for? How did yer earn yer clout?

BOY

Burnt papers he were saving to cut out.

OLD MAN

What papers?

BOY

All t'*Posts* and *Stars* wi' bits

about 'em closing down t'bloody pits.

OLD MAN

He'd not usually clout thee, would thi dad.

He's laid off after today and he feels bad.

BOY

He chucked my schoolbook into t'fire an all!

OLD MAN

He's lost his job, love! He feels small.

BOY *and* OLD MAN *fall silent.*

55. INT. MIRROR ROOM, KIRKBY MAIN COLLIERY, DAY

DAD *looks at himself in a mirror which has on it:* THIS MAN IS RESPONSIBLE FOR YOUR SAFETY. *He greets his reflection with a wry smile, which fades rapidly.*

56. EXT. LIMITS OF 'CONTRABAND ZONE', COLLIERY, DAY

MINERS *are taking their last drags on their cigarettes. The wall behind them is painted in red and white warning stripes over which is printed in large black capitals:* CONTRABAND ZONE.

A pit-boot grinds out the last cigarette.

The word CONTRABAND *is left as a* MINER *leaves the frame.*

57. INT. ENTRANCE TO PIT-CAGE, DAY

HERMES, *this time in the gear of a colliery Tallyman awaits the arrival*

*of the last shift. There is a contemptuous anticipation on his face as we
hear the* MINERS *approaching.*

The MINERS *give the Tallyman one of their tallies. As each does this
he whispers under his breath:* Cunt!

MINERS *enter the cage.* HERMES *(Tallyman) lets down the metal
screen over the cage and the cage door closes. As the cage descends all the*
MINERS *shout together:* Cunt!

HERMES *looks down the shaft with great contempt and speaks in
ancient Greek the following lines from Aeschylus,* Prometheus Bound,
976–8:

HERMES

σε τον σοφιστην, τον πικρως υπερπικρον
τον᾽ εξαμαρτοντ᾽ ες θεους εφημεροις
ποροντα τιμας, τον πυρος κλεπτην λεγω.

HERMES *chinks the twelve tallies in his hand as he walks away.*

58. INT. MIRROR ROOM, DAY
HERMES *regards himself in the mirror over which is written:* THIS MAN
IS RESPONSIBLE FOR YOUR SAFETY.

HERMES

You never expected I could speak
so fluently in ancient Greek.
Well, the truth is that I can
because I'm a god, and not a man.

HERMES *throws the twelve Miners' tallies to the ground. He appears as
a naked silver statue in the mirror, and then in human form in a silver
suit with his caduceus in his hand.*

HERMES

And why, you might ask, should gods come
into this world of ' 'Ee-by-gum'?
Those dropped aitches help disguise
the fact I've flown down from the skies.
Just as steel-capped boots conceal
the wings that sprout out of each heel.
I hid the fact, by talking broad,
that I'm a posh Olympian lord.
It took just a few 'by 'eckers like's

PHIL HUNT

19

and 'ecky thumps' to con these Tykes
into believing that this god
was just a fellow Northern sod,
playing darts and dominoes
and, Zeus help me, speaking *prose*!
I mean an immortal, Hermes, me,
not spouting proper poetry!

59. INT. CONTRABAND SIGN, MIRROR ROOM, COLLIERY, DAY
The shadow of the caduceus of HERMES *passes across a white sign with
red letters reading:*
National Coal Board – North Eastern Division – No.2
(Doncaster) Area
CONTRABAND
ANY PERSON WHO TAKES CONTRABAND BELOW GROUND AT
THIS MINE, OR IS IN POSSESSION OF CONTRABAND BELOW
GROUND, OR IS FOUND IN POSSESSION OF CONTRABAND ON
BEING SEARCHED WHEN ABOUT TO GO BELOW GROUND IS
LIABLE TO BE SUMMARILY DISMISSED FROM HIS EMPLOYMENT
AND DEBARRED FROM SUBSEQUENT EMPLOYMENT IN THE
INDUSTRY.
SUCH PERSONS MAY ALSO BE PROSECUTED UNDER THE MINES
AND QUARRIES ACT.
CONTRABAND INCLUDES ANY CIGAR OR CIGARETTE, ANY PIPE
OR OTHER CONTRIVANCE FOR SMOKING, OR ANY MATCH OR
MECHANICAL LIGHTER.

60. EXT. PIT WINDING GEAR, DAY
The wheels of the pit winding gear spin and groan to a creaky halt.

61. EXT. SPOIL HEAPS, COLLIERY, DAY
HERMES *walks on the colliery spoil heaps, speaking:*

HERMES
This is the *terminus ad quem*
for bolshy bastards such as them.
Terminus ad quem and that in
local lingo, not in Latin,
the language into which one slips
when one's a god, means ' 'ad their chips!'
In local lingo, note, gods rhyme

effortlessly all the time.
Poetry of this posh sort'll
never come from a mere mortal.
It's quite beyond mere mortal reach,
this pure Olympian form of speech.
It's a pure Olympian privilege
forbidden folk from Ferrybridge.
Olympians who serve Zeus speak
(apart from fluent ancient Greek)
such local lingos as one needs
when slumming it in Hull or Leeds.
And local lingos gods transform
by giving them poetic form.

HERMES *walks up a sloping stretch of the spoil heap. The sound of a*
groaning dumper truck.

62. EXT. COLLIERY, RAILWAY LOADING BAY, DAY
A dumper truck tips a load of coal into a rail container linked to
others in a seemingly endless line. In the right foreground is a red
metal box reading: FIRE HOSE.
  The sound of a match being struck.

63. INT. WRECKED BUS, DAY
The sound of the striking match came from the OLD MAN *lighting up a*
cigarette. He leans back exhaling smoke, ready for the 'journey'.

BOY
  But I have to tell yer even an old bloke,
  has to go upstairs if he wants to smoke.
OLD MAN
  Them stairs 'll bloody kill me with my cough.
BOY (*becoming 'official'*)
  You must either smoke upstairs, sir, or get off.

64. EXT. WRECKING YARD, DAY
OLD MAN *gets off, coughing.*

OLD MAN
  What are you talking like that for?
BOY
  Like what?

OLD MAN
          Like a bloody panto!
BOY
                              No, I'm not!
OLD MAN
     You are! You're rhyming like that geezer
     in *Aladdin*, Uncle Ebeneezer!
BOY
     *A*ban*a*zar! *A*ban*a*zar! Ebeneezer's *Scrooge*.
OLD MAN
     We sound like t'comic and his stooge.

OLD MAN *drags on his cigarette and contemplates the shadows of steam drifting across the cooling towers. His boots rest on an old chain.*

OLD MAN
     I suppose it suits the bloody time
     when Britain's one long pantomime,
     where t' workers have been bloody conned
     and someone waves a sodding wand
     and down comes all the winding gear
     that's stood in place a hundred year.
     Them Tories twisting and two-timing . . .
     Tha's got me at it, bloody rhyming.
     Stop it!
BOY
          Can't help it!
OLD MAN
                         Bloody try!
BOY
     You mean try talking normal.
OLD MAN
                              Ay!
BOY
     It's thee an' all. You spoiled it then
     by saying Ay.
OLD MAN
          Well, I won't again.

They look at each other, aware that they are still rhyming.

OLD MAN

Gi' us a lift to t'pictures then. I'll pay.
Ah bet fare's rocketed since my day.
It cost a penny then from here to there.

BOY

A penny? It's 20p now, t'single fare.

OLD MAN

Ah've got us bus pass. Ah don't 'ave to pay.

BOY

Show us it!

OLD MAN *fishes out bus pass.*

BOY

Sit down, then, OK!

BOY *begins to 'drive' bus.*

BOY

Brrrm-brrrm-brrrm . . .

VOICE OF HERMES

Constant theft! First fire, now this –
pinching poetic artifice!
How can Olympus stay intact
if *poetry* comes to *Pontefract*?

BOY

Brrrm! Brrrm! Brrrm!

OLD MAN

By 'eck, lad, this bus is bloody slow.
At this rate I'll be missing t'picture show.
I'll walk there under mi own steam.
Stay in your broken bus and dream.

BOY

Tha can talk, grandad. Tha's never seen
a single picture on that Palace screen.
It closed down forty year ago.

OLD MAN

I'm off, or else I'll miss mi show.
Don't tell thi grandma where I am.
And I'll not tell on thee. She's mad, thi mam.
I'll not let on that tha's been skiving.

23

Or that tha's got no licence and tha's driving.

BOY *and* OLD MAN *make a silent agreement to connive.*
OLD MAN *stares at the shadows of steam across the barrel of the
cooling towers above them as if looking for inspiration there.*
Then out to BOY, *cheerfully back in his dream of the 'pictures'.*

OLD MAN
I'll get missen some humbugs or a piece
of liquorice . . .
BOY
                              And, me, I'm off to Greece.
OLD MAN
Send us a postcard.
BOY
                        Ay, and you enjoy
your Ginger Rogers and her brother Roy!
(*to himself:*) Barmy!
OLD MAN (*overhearing as he walks away*)
                              If I'm barmy so are thee.
Birds of a barmy feather, thee and me.

OLD MAN *looks at the shadows on the cooling tower. He lights up a
cigarette and walks out of the wrecked bus yard, dominated by the
cooling towers. He coughs.*
BOY *drives bus.*

65. EXT. AERIAL SHOT, COOLING TOWERS, DAY

VOICE OF HERMES
What my boss Zeus longed to do
was melt Man down and mould a new,
smelt the old stock and recast
a better Mankind from the last.

66. EXT. CHURCHYARD, DAY
OLD MAN *continues his walk through a graveyard dominated by the
power station cooling towers. Breathless and coughing, he leans on a
stone cross. In the distance behind him is the winding gear of the colliery.*

VOICE OF HERMES
And 'better' was his way of saying

Man with a bent for more obeying.
Zeus would have fulfilled his dreams
but for Prometheus and his schemes,
whose theft of fire first blurred the line
dividing Mankind and divine,
letting lower challenge higher
by giving mere men Zeus's fire.

67. EXT. WRECKING YARD, DAY

The BOY *'drives' his bus. Then he leaves the bus and enters a fire-engine. He is deep in thought about his burnt book and the row with his Dad. Shadows of steam on cooling towers. Then he breaks his mood and imitates the fire-engine siren, 'driving' it at break-neck speed. He pulls the lever of the cracked bell on the roof of the wrecked fire-engine.*

The cracked bell keeps tolling.

PHIL HUNT

68. EXT. STREET, PALACE CINEMA, KNOTTINGLEY, DAY

OLD MAN *takes his walk to the Palace Cinema past various locations dominated by the cooling towers until, with the cooling towers behind him, we see him coming up the street towards the cinema.*

He has a secret entrance into the derelict cinema. He looks round, stubs out a cigarette, and enters.

69. INT. PALACE CINEMA, DAY

There are one or two scattered stall seats left in the ruin, one of which is the OLD MAN *'s favourite.*

We see his face look at the screen, lighten up when he sees that there is an image, then darken when he sees that it is HERMES *entering the bootroom of Kirkby Main Colliery.*

He sits in his seat and lights up.

Cut to:

70. INT. COLLIERY, BOOT MACHINE CORRIDOR, DAY

HERMES *goes into his fire-precaution routine and addresses the audience to this film and the solitary figure of the* OLD MAN *in the derelict Palace Cinema.*

HERMES
Though fire, we don't have any doubt,
has little chance of breaking out,
nonetheless the laws require
your cinema to plan for fire,
so before this film proceeds too far
please check *now* where the Exits are.
Since fire's what this film's about,
you ought to know a quick way out!
Turn your eyes left, turn your eyes right
and note the nearest Exit light,
on either side in red or green.

Audiences in cinema hopefully go through the cautionary procedure.

How obedient you've been!

71. INT. PALACE CINEMA, DAY

The OLD MAN *is the one spectator, sitting on one of the few seats left, chain-smoking.*

OLD MAN
Bollocks! I've known where
t'Exits are for fifty year!
HERMES (*on the tattered screen in black and white*)
But even a venerable sire
of seventy years must watch for fire.

HERMES *turns politely but icily stern with the* **OLD MAN,** *who is dragging deeply on his cigarette.*

HERMES
   And may we remind our clientele
   they make not smoke.
OLD MAN (*puffing away*)
                     Like bloody 'ell!

He takes another ostentatious puff.

   That's when I stopped bloody going
   oo matter what great flick were showing.
   If it were a Cagney or a Bogart on
   even then I wouldn't'a gone.
   No, when fags were finally forbidden
   in this rat-infested and flea-ridden
   bug'utch, bugger it, I thought,
   I'll bloody smoke and not get caught.
   I smoked, got caught, and allus chucked
   out on mi lug'ole. Films were fucked.
   I just stopped seeing picture shows.

NICK WALL

27

T'whole bloody place all full of NOS:
no bloody smoking, spitting, booze,
no even lighting up in t'loos.
Ay, I bloody tried that too,
having a quiet drag in t'loo.
But t'old maid wi' her ice-cream tray
saw t'smoke and gave the game away.
I smoked that fast it made a fug
and got me chucked out on mi lug.
Then I said, 'Sod it! That's me done!'
Forbidding fags spoiled all my fun.

In t'pit and t'flea-pit cigarettes
were contraband to these tight gets.
Underground makes sense. But bloody 'ell
banning fags in t'flicks as well!
Sometimes I think t' whole bloody land
's made bloody baccy contraband.

When Bogey lit up so did I,
smoke curling past my one closed eye.
Bogey gets best smoker's prize,
cig-smoke crinkling up his eyes.

OLD MAN *demonstrates.*

All t' gangsters had a swirling cloak
cast all around 'em in thick smoke.
When they inhaled their smoke I did
and so did every other kid,
when they exhaled so did a crowd
of kids, synchronized in one huge cloud.
So it were no fun if I weren't free
to light my fag with Edward G.
And summat these days tha don't get 's
heroes smoking cigarettes.
I'd love to rerun every bit
of bloody film where fags get lit.
I'd like to watch a thousand clips
of ciggies dangling from wet lips,
the mean lips of Chicago hoods

on corners in bleak neighbourhoods,
loitering in dark parts of town
to gun some other gangster down,
them painted scarlet lips that pout
to blow some perfect smoke-rings out,
what I now know as prostitutes
with six-inch heels who smoked cheroots.
Brilliant the way pairs broke
the ice between 'em with a smoke!

Who smokes now? Them were the days
when women smoked in negligées.
Those elegant and high-heeled dames
leaning into men's match-flames,
too close for comfort, with their eyes
locked rock-steady on the guy's,
then that first stream of exhaled smoke
blown straight into the gob-smacked bloke.
I learned cig-skills from what I'd seen
sexy smokers do on t'screen.

HERMES *looks contemptuously from the black and white screen.*

I were convinced that good cig-suction
were t' secret weapon of seduction.
It seemed that shared cigs allus led
them passionate puffers off to bed.
And when you knew they'd had their shag
first thing both did were light a fag!

And have a fag 's what I do here
in memory of yesteryear.
'Cos now this place is derelict
I can't get chucked out, nabbed or nicked
for smoking all them fags their law
wouldn't let me smoke afore.
I come here now to treat missen
to all them fags not dragged on then.

OLD MAN *looks down at his feet: CU of hundreds of fag-ends. The
memory of forbidden fags makes him defiant.*

OLD MAN *rises from his seat into the pose of Prometheus, the fist in defiance of the image of* HERMES *in black and white on the tattered screen.*

OLD MAN
Smokers of the world unite!

He speaks to the audiences at whatever cinemas Prometheus *is shown.*

On t'count o' three, all light up, right?
1–2–3 . . .

He's disappointed.

You've all been cowed.
I've changed the law and it's allowed.
Try again then. 1–2–3:
all light your fags now after me.

OLD MAN *lights his cigarette, inhales deeply with defiant satisfaction, then collapses coughing into his seat. It takes him some time to recover.*

72. INT. COLLIERY, BOOT-CLEANING MACHINE, DAY

HERMES
Before that clapped-out cloth-capped sod
dared interrupt this ancient god,
I was explaining Zeus's plan
to finish off the world of Man
was foiled by the Promethean theft
for men like him with one lung left
who flaunt the filched fire day and night
by keeping cigarettes alight.
This angers Zeus, but all that smoke
'll make that cancerous codger croak,
so Zeus is gratified how fire that first
made Man euphoric's now reversed,
watching this Fire-thief supporter
's breath get short and ever shorter,
not Armageddon but still fun
to watch men dying one by one,
especially from ills Man gets

from coal-face work or cigarettes!
The day Zeus tires of the joke
he'll wipe the lot out at one stroke.
Smog, pollution, smoker's cough
might do as well to bring that off.
So Armageddon's put on hold
till Zeus is bored or Man too bold.
Zeus loves the ozone layer in shreds
and slumming it in human beds!

HERMES *looks down at his elegant silver boots, which are smirched by his walk on the spoil heap.*

This filthy slag-shit scarcely suits
one's svelte gods-wear silver boots.
After my god's toe this machine
'll brush no more men's pit-boots clean.

73. EXT. COLLIERY WINDING GEAR, DAY
Still winding gear creaks into life. Cut to:

74. INT. PIT CAGE, DAY
Pit cage ascending and gates opening. Twelve MINERS *stand stunned by what they see. It is as if they have been underground for years. The mine is deserted and in ruins.*

75. EXT. DERELICT COLLIERY, DAY
The pit is deserted, and totally derelict. Doors fallen down. The mirror with the THIS MAN IS RESPONSIBLE FOR YOUR SAFETY *inscription: a* MINER *stares at it in reflection, then a chunk of falling rubble shatters it.*
    A fire bucket still full of water falls, settles and rocks, slopping its water.
    The red and white bricks that made the wall announcing the CONTRABAND ZONE: *a partial section of the wall reads* CON.
    Half a headgear wheel falls.
    As the MINERS *walk forward astonished, plaster falls from the roof. It seems that the place is about to fall down. The cage door falls and breaks a pillar. The* MINERS *run down a corridor of rubble and tangled machinery and straight into a cattle-truck.*
    The silver STATUE OF HERMES *points his caduceus.*

76. EXT. CATTLE-TRUCK, DAY
The back of the cattle-truck of KRATOS *and* BIA *is slammed shut and bolted by a hand in black rubber gloves.*

77. INT. CATTLE-TRUCK, DAY
Through the slats of the cattle-truck the MINERS *see the cooling towers. The truck starts up, throwing some* MINERS *onto the floor.*

MINER 1
Hey, bloody hell fire!
MINER 2
What the fuck!
MINER 3
Where the 'ell 're we off to, take a look.

78. EXT. AI BRIDGE OVER CANAL, DAY
The cattle-truck speeds over the bridge dominated by cooling towers.

MINER 4
Just crossing t'bridge that goes over t'canal.
And there's barge with thi brother on it, Mal.
Shove thi gob through here. Give him a yell.

79. EXT. CANAL NEAR BRIDGE, DAY
A barge is about to pass under the bridge where the truck is passing. Voice of MINER 5 *shouting* Brian! Brian!

80. INT. CATTLE-TRUCK, DAY

MINER 5
Brian! Brian?
MINER 4
Did he hear you?
MINER 5
Did 'e 'ell!

81. EXT. AI NEAR POWER STATION, DAY
The truck passes the cooling towers. Pan with truck as it heads down motorway, and hold on sign reading: AI THE SOUTH.

82. EXT. CANAL, DAY
Cut back to barge and CU of wake of barge churning water, which mixes into:

83. INT. OCEANUS FISH FACTORY, DAY

CU of fish in bubbling water. Pan up to fish emerging from water on conveyor.

HERMES *in the overalls of an Oceanus foreman driving a fork-lift truck enters the tank room, glances at the struggling fish and drives on through a heavy blue plastic curtain.*

HERMES (*driving fork-lift*)
Zeus always wanted the entire
plays of Aeschylus destroyed by fire,
Aeschylus's . . .

HERMES *realizes that no one in the cinema audience has any idea who Aeschylus is.*

OK! Stop!
You! With the popcorn and the pop!
who don't (perhaps!) already know it,
Aeschylus, the great Greek poet,
died (by one of Zeus's tricks!)
in the year Four Fifty Six,
that's BC, and he sang the praise
of bloody Prometheus in his plays.
Especially one that's still around
and famous as *Prometheus Bound*.
And that play with its rebel views in
needs spin-doctoring and defusing.
And that's where my slick skills come in.
I'm employed to give Zeus spin.
And making statues is the way
I've chosen to defuse that play.
For which I now create my cast
I swear to Zeus will be the last.

HERMES *drives through another blue plastic curtain with some of the Oceanus* WOMEN *standing on the pallet. Then another curtain and more women. The fork-lift emerges through the final hanging blue plastic curtain out to the loading bay. As they pass through the curtain the* WOMEN *all sing a high sustained note, which is smothered as a cloth of blue silk falls over them. Their shapes, heads and arms, struggle under the cloth and then freeze.*

33

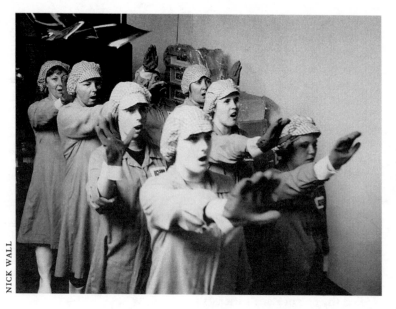

NICK WALL

Three heads covered with blue cloth fill the frame. Then mix to:

84. EXT. HUMBER ESTUARY AND BRIDGE, DAY
The blue cloth begins to billow and flutter and we pull back to reveal a drifting pontoon approaching the Humber Bridge with shapes covered by the cloth.

The blue cloth blows into the air. The shapes are revealed as the Daughters of Ocean.

HERMES *is on a vantage point on the bridge watching them approach slowly.*

85. EXT. HUMBER ESTUARY AND BRIDGE, DAY
The DAUGHTERS OF OCEAN *nearer the Bridge.*

HERMES
    This choir's just Zeus's little quirk.
    They handled scales so well at work.
    What sport to squeeze these lumpen proles
    into the choral corset of posh roles,
    to warble a mournful little number
    as they start drifting down the Humber,

just as their menfolk start their route
to death down a scrap metal chute,
and drift through Europe all the way
to Elefsina for my play,
bewailing the dire fate that falls
on Fire-grabber, Golden-balls.
I promise you that we'll require
the sweetener service of a choir
when men go shrieking in the fire.

The hand of HERMES *with its nails painted silver plucks a cable of the Humber Bridge and it gives out a Humberside-wide bass note.*

86. INT. PALACE CINEMA, DAY
OLD MAN *is woken from a nap by the note of the Humber Bridge.*

87. EXT. HUMBER BRIDGE, SPIDERMAN WALKWAY ACCESS GATE, DAY
HERMES *opens the gate to the curved spiderman walkway to the tower of the Humber Bridge.*

HERMES
When I'm not in human guise
this little lyre's about my size.
I'll walk up on my god-size lyre
that gives the note that starts my choir.
For ages now I've longed to strum
my Humber harp/harmonium.

HERMES *closes the metal door of the walkway. It sends out a huge reverberant note, which is picked up by the* DAUGHTERS OF OCEAN *on the Humber.* HERMES *smiles with satisfaction.*
   HERMES *begins to climb the rest of the walkway. The 'strings' of the Humber Bridge lyre continue to reverberate as he climbs to the top.*
   Cut to:

88. EXT. TOWER WALKWAY, DAY
As the cattle-truck moves towards the Humber Bridge, HERMES *is revealed in a central commanding position on the tower walkway of the bridge.*

HERMES (*on tower*)
   Now let my god-size Yorkshire lyre
   descant on all the doom of FIRE!

HERMES *'conducts' with a slow, measured movement of his caduceus. A vast, eery, reverberant hum comes from the 'lyre' (Humber Bridge), and the* DAUGHTERS OF OCEAN *harmonize around the hum.*

89. INT. CATTLE-TRUCK, DAY
The reverberant hum of the Humber Bridge 'lyre' and the voices of the DAUGHTERS OF OCEAN *singing something infinitely sad is heard by the* MINERS *in the truck.*

MINER 5
   That's a bloody creepy noise off t'sea.
MINER 3
   Sounds like a funeral dirge to me.

CUs of MINERS' *faces puzzled and rather frightened by the singing. They fall silent as the dirge recedes.*

MINER 1
   Have you noticed summat?
MINER 2
                          What?
MINER 1
                                    Every time
   we make a sentence it ends up wi' a rhyme!
MINER 3
   I'm not joining in, I'm not, old son.
MINER 5
   Except someone'll complete what you've begun!
   Like I've just gone and done it now missen!
MINER 6
   So what do you think 's happening to us then?
MINER 5
   God knows, but t' bloody world goes speeding by.
MINER 6
   Are we off South?
MINER 5 (*looking through slats*)
                     Looks like it. Ay!

36

MINER 1
>An t'barmiest thing of all 's like when
>we talk in bloody rhyme like I did then.
>I don't like it. It's more than bloody queer
>spouting bloody poetry like King Lear.

MINER 3
>It could well launch us on a new career.
>Did you hear that? Did you hear me?
>It just came out like that, rhyme no. 3.
>Hey, now we're redundant, we could all go
>to bloody Blackpool as a Pierrot show.

The MINERS *are unresponsive.*

90. EXT. MOTORWAY, DUSK
*The cattle-truck is seen from a motorway bridge among heavy traffic. It
passes under the bridge.*

91. INT. CATTLE-TRUCK, NIGHT
MINERS' *POV from inside truck of receding gas station and laughing
attendant.*

92. EXT. CHANNEL FERRY HARBOUR, DAY
The cattle-truck approaches the open hatch of a ferry.

VOICE OF HERMES
>And now they go across rough sea
>into my scrap-heap *pot-pourri,*
>the last ingredients for the pan
>part scrap metal, part scrap man,
>the fag-end of the Fire-thief's soul
>stirred into my mixture whole.
>
>Fag-end Prometheans cock no snook,
>confined in their own piss and puke.
>So, with your bowels and bladders full
>bid your fond farewells to ' 'ull'!

93. INT. CATTLE-TRUCK, FERRY, DAY
Bars of light across the faces of MINERS *are extinguished as the ferry
hatch closes slowly. The fluorescent light in the hold falls onto one* MINER
who is looking decidedly queasy. MINER 2 *notices that he looks sea-sick.*

MINER 1

Puke into your helmet, then we'll slop
t' whole lot out when t'buggers stop,
after we've landed, for a piss or drink.

MINER 2

It's already too much is this stink.
Some bugger I could bloody hit
's gone and done a secret shit.

The sea-sick MINER *pukes, but onto the top of his helmet, not inside it.*

MINER 3 (*taking charge*)

Right! Anyone who has to go
has to use his helmet as a po.
Then shove it peak first through t'truck slat
and slop the contents out, like that.
Show some discipline. Then we'll dispose
on t'open road of all t'full pos.
Turds tha'll have to spike and flick
through t'slats, and if tha's sick
puke into t'helmet, chuck it, vomit
's got a bloody foul stink from it.

MINER 4

Making poetry out of stuff like this!
Tha's t'bloody Shakespeare of puke and piss.
I never thought I'd hear an ode
on DIYing a commode.

94. EXT. AUTOBAHN, GERMANY, DAY
The cattle-truck turns off a German autobahn.

95. INT. CATTLE-TRUCK, NIGHT
Headlights of oncoming trucks and cars send bars of light into the cattle-truck, revealing sickly looking captive passengers, all awake, staring.

One steadies a slopping helmet. As the truck stops at a service station the helmet's contents slop over. The MINERS *leap to their feet to avoid the spillage.*

96. INT. CATTLE-TRUCK, SERVICE STATION, BERLIN–DRESDEN,
NIGHT

MINER 4 (*sudden dark despair*)
  I can't stand much more of this.
MINER 2
                                        I smell pizza!
MINER 6
                                                        I smell piss.
MINER 5 (*listening at slats*)
  Germany! I can just make out
  that t'lingo that they're talking's Kraut.

97. EXT. FOUNDRY, NIGHT
The cattle-truck turns off the autobahn towards a vast industrial plant.
  The cattle-truck tips the MINERS *onto a chute, which leads into a
cauldron of molten metal.*

98. INT. FOUNDRY CHUTE, NIGHT
Frightened screams.
  Fingernails scraping rust off the chute as the MINERS *try to stop
sliding.*
  Helmets and boots sink into the fiery porridge.
  A helmet melts. Shrill, terrifying screaming, clouds of smoke.
  MINER 4, *the last to enter the fiery cauldron, slides towards the fire
with a blood-curdling scream.*
  *Then an almost peaceful 'liquid' music (Daughters of Ocean) as we
cut to:*
  *A trickle of gold running down a channel towards the mould which
will create the Statue of Prometheus.*
  Someone in the same costume as KRATOS *and* BIA *scrapes away a
little sand and reveals the golden fist of the* STATUE OF PROMETHEUS.

VOICE OF HERMES
  Miners from that molten muck 'll
  melt into each golden knuckle.
  A fag-end Prometheus still exists
  in their recycled strikers' fists.

99. EXT. FOUNDRY, DAWN
A vast door like an aeroplane hangar with the fire-forbidden logo.

39

The golden STATUE OF PROMETHEUS *made of melted-down miners comes out of the foundry to a fanfare. The whole statue is swathed in red-and-white hazard tape, as if mummified. In the left hand is a blazing torch.*

HERMES *stops the truck, raising his caduceus like a traffic cop. He gets* FORCE *and* VIOLENCE *to climb onto the truck and tear the blazing torch from the left hand of Prometheus.*

A boot stamps on the burning end of the statue's fennel stalk.

IOO. INT. PALACE CINEMA, DAY
OLD MAN *looks at his cigarette.*

IOI. EXT. FOUNDRY, DAY
The caduceus of HERMES *indicates the direction of the truck and statue.*
    Cut to:

IO2. EXT. ROAD IN GERMANY, DAY
The STATUE OF PROMETHEUS *travelling along a road in Germany. As it moves, the hazard tape begins to unwrap and flap and is gradually ripped off by the wind, revealing the golden statue. Hazard tape snags on trees and telegraph poles, etc.*

CUs of flapping tape and bits of the radiant golden giant.

The STATUE OF PROMETHEUS *sheds its final length of hazard tape and is revealed in all its glory.*

IO3. EXT. BERLIN–DRESDEN ROAD, DAY
A Dresden fire-fighter truck overtakes the STATUE OF PROMETHEUS *with its lights flashing and its siren wailing.*

The noise of the fire-truck siren becomes the noise made by the BOY *driving his wrecked fire-truck in the Ferrybridge wrecking yard.*

IO4. EXT. WRECKING YARD, DAY

BOY
    Errr! Errr! Err!

We hear the BOY *making his fire-engine sounds, then mix back to the sound of the Dresden fire-truck's siren as it overtakes the* STATUE OF PROMETHEUS *on the road to Dresden.*

IO5. EXT. DRESDEN ROAD, DAY
Dresden fire-truck reveals sign saying DRESDEN. *Statue disappearing in distance.*

The caduceus taps the DRESDEN *sign. Pull back to reveal* HERMES, *sweeping his caduceus in the direction of the* STATUE OF PROMETHEUS *heading for Dresden.*

VOICE OF HERMES
    With the new millennium nigh
    Zeus wants his forces standing by
    to make one final all-out thrust
    to grind Prometheus into dust.
    And Dresden, city of destructive flame,
    's the best for blackening his good name.
    Those 35,000 fire flayed
    won't cheer Prometheus on parade.
    Nor will their descendants cheer
    when we take Prometheus here.

107. EXT. CAROLABRUCKE, DRESDEN, DAY
The STATUE OF PROMETHEUS *crosses the Carolabrucke from the Albertplatz and Albertstrasse direction towards the Albertinum.*

VOICE OF HERMES
> I'll make them so rue fire that men'll
> want to fuck him with his fennel.
> 35,000 in two days
> perished in the Dresden blaze.
> Even though the targets then
> were blasphemous icons more than men,

108. INT. PALACE CINEMA, DAY

HERMES (*from the screen*)
> Promethean icons Zeus's ire
> wanted blasting in the fire.

OLD MAN (*to* HERMES *on the screen*)
> I want to see t'newsreels that I saw
> on Saturday mornings during t'War.
> And show us what were justly done
> by Bomber Harris to the Hun.
> When Bomber Harris turned on t'heat
> I cheered it from this very seat.
> You should have heard t'whole Palace roar
> to see the Gerries get what for.
> T'whole Palace bug'utch cheered and clapped
> when . . .

HERMES (*completing his couplet on the tattered screen*)
> . . . my master Zeus had Dresden zapped!

The OLD MAN *stares at* HERMES *on the screen.*

109. EXT. SEMPER OPER, DRESDEN, DAY

HERMES
> Zeus gutted this. To know the cause,
> come through the Semper Oper's doors
> though I advise a moment's pause
> to reflect on Zeus and let reflection
> awe you into genuflection.

HERMES *duly genuflects to the relief of Zeus.*

110. INT. PALACE CINEMA, DAY
OLD MAN *sits staring at the relief of Zeus.*

OLD MAN
> I'll tell thee summat. I'm not awed
> by any bloody overlord.
> In Yorkshire we've got us own sign
> when we're saluting owt divine.

OLD MAN *makes a v-sign and raspberry noise at Zeus.*
On the screen the hand of HERMES *with silver-painted finger-nails strokes the eagle of Zeus on the same relief. As his hand strokes and moves down the body of the eagle the* OLD MAN *coughs, and the defiant v-sign crumples as he's wracked by coughing.*
HERMES *enters the Semper Oper.*

III. INT. SEMPER OPER, DRESDEN, DAY
HERMES *shows us the painted lunette of Prometheus chained to the rock.*

VOICE OF HERMES
> Though now the damned thing's been redone
> this was Zeus's target number 1.

II2. EXT. SEMPER OPER, SMOKE-BLACKENED STATUE OF PROMETHEUS

VOICE OF HERMES (*continuing*)
> And target 2, Prometheus, black
> from the bomb-Blitz blaze, but back
> on the Opera as he was before
> the Allies bombed him in the War,
> reinstated where his gaze
> once watched the whole of Dresden blaze.
> (Here is Dresden's true destroyer
> filthy from his own filched *Feuer!*)

II3. EXT. ZWINGER PALACE, DRESDEN, RELIEF OF PROMETHEUS FREED BY HERCULES

VOICE OF HERMES (*continuing*)
> And target 3, much worse, this frieze:
> Prometheus freed by Hercules,
> who shot an arrow from his quiver
> through the bird that gnawed the liver

43

of Prometheus, and now comes to rend
the lungs of our fag-flaunting friend.
Unlike the Titan's liver though
his lungs aren't likely to regrow.
This pitiful, pulmonary prole
carves scrap-heap miners out of coal,
conniving in that blasphemy
that it wasn't Zeus at all but he,
Prometheus, who formed man from clay,
target 4, that, to this day
Dresden flaunts up here, restored,
provoking my Olympian Lord.

114. EXT. KUNSTSCHULE, DRESDEN, RELIEF OF AESCHYLUS

VOICE OF HERMES (*continuing*)
And that same eagle also split
the skull of Aeschylus, the poet-shit,
and shattered the bald pate when it dropped
a tortoise from the sky, and stopped
the blasphemous poetic flow
some two millennia ago,
Aeschylus, pro-Promethean bard,
back up in Dresden, with beard charred,
and with a layer of fire-storm soot
like a skinhead haircut on his nut.
If Zeus were with me, what he'd do
is give this poet a piss shampoo.
Zeus likes to pump his pungent pee
all over poets and poetry.
First burst to Aeschylus, then squirt a
shower on Shakespeare, Schiller, Goethe.
Poets have taught Mankind to breach
the boundaries Zeus put round speech,
and the fire Prometheus stole
created man's poetic soul.

115. EXT. RIVER NEAR AUGUSTUSBRUCKE, DRESDEN, DAY
The boy's MAM, *who has run across Europe, collecting wood and paper
to make a fire under the bridge.*

44

VOICE OF HERMES (*continuing*)
> The Yorkshire mam! She'll always hear
> the boots of KRATOS and of BIA.
> Force and Violence get their fun
> keeping the poor cow on the run.
> This is the cow I've let them hound
> like IO in *Prometheus Bound.*

> Poor KRATOS and his sidekick BIA
> miss the swastikas of yesteryear.
> They've come to Dresden and they've sighed
> for the good old days of genocide.
> How they've yearned to reinstate
> the furnace as a people's fate.

> KRATOS and BIA*'s R & R's*
> *more butch barbarity than bars,*
> *and so to keep them entertained*
> *until I get Prometheus chained,*
> *I've let them have her as their toy*
> *to drive demented then destroy.*
> *To death, through Dresden from Doncaster*
> *dogged and hounded, faster, faster,*
> *she'll suffer, this fire-kindling Frau,*
> (in the likeness of a Friesian cow),
> the sort of fate that's been assigned
> to those considered not one's kind,
> those hate's gadflies force to flee,
> schizophrenic, gypsy, refugee.
> They'll turn the screw of paranoia
> then, fun done, finish her in . . . *Feuer.*

> She now thinks of *Feuer* as her friend
> where thousands met a fiery end.

116. EXT. FOOTBALL STADIUM, DAY
The STATUE OF PROMETHEUS *centred in the Dresden football
stadium.* HERMES *uses his caduceus to bring on the great floodlights,
which glare at the Statue like interrogation lights.*

45

HERMES
  Now to summon up the choir
  of thousands perished in the fire.

With his caduceus HERMES *summons up the ghosts of those who died in
the Dresden fire-storm of 13–14 February, 1945. They rouse as drones
from different stands in the stadium.*

  HERMES *first points the caduceus at the North stand. From the dark,
empty stand comes a drone composed of voices and RAF bombers
carrying their loads to shed over Dresden.*

  *A whisper of the voices of the dead comes through the drone. They are
whispering their names:*

NORTH CHOIR
  Zeilig, Albin
  Grafe, Bruno
  Lachmann, Frida
  Mehnert, Rolf
  Kuhnscharf, Walter . . .

HERMES *points his caduceus to the empty South stand. The drone is
heard in stereo as more names join those being whispered from the North
stand.*

SOUTH CHOIR
  Dietz, Jurgen
  Schroter, Hans
  Hennig, Annerose
  Mühler . . .

HERMES *points his caduceus at the West stand and more voices swell
the growing counterpoint. Then he points his caduceus at the East stand
and the drone swells to a crescendo, which leads to the* CHORUS OF
GHOSTS, *singing in unison the words of two witnesses who, like many
thousands, were burned or asphyxiated in the cellars where they took
refuge from the fire-storm.*

CHORUS OF GHOSTS
  Wir sassen im Keller
  Wartend auf den Tod.
  Das Haus brannte
  in Keller lief Phosphor.

Over the drone THREE BOYS *sing with the* CHOIR OF GHOSTS. *Boys 1 and 3 carry charred, buckled old Dresden street signs: one reads* Holbeinstrasse, *the other* Goethestrasse.

BOY 1
Kreuzkirche, wo ich sange,
Zerstort.
BOY 2
Kreuzschule, wo ich studierte,
Zerstort.
BOY 3
Kreuzstrasse, wo ich spielte
Zerstort.
BOYS 1, 2, 3 (*overlapping*)
Kreuzkirche, Dornkirche, Frauenkirche,
Wo wir sangen,
Zerstort.

Kreuzschule, Hochschule, Oberschule,
Wo wir studierten,
Zerstort.

Kreuzstrasse, Durerstrasse, Rosenstrasse,
Wo wir spielten,
Zerstort.

The CHORUS OF GHOSTS *takes up the list of Dresden streets gutted by the fire.*

CHORUS OF GHOSTS
Durerstrasse, Cranachstrasse, Holbeinstrasse,
Goethestrasse, Webergasse, Albrechtstrasse,
Christianstrasse, Friedrichstrasse, Alter Markt,
Johannesstrasse, Mathildenstrasse, Marienstrasse,
Pragerstrasse, Munchenstrasse, Ziegelstrasse,
Zinzendorfstrasse, Pirnaischestrasse, Zirkusstrasse.

117. INT. PALACE CINEMA, DAY
Archive film of the Dresden bombing is seen on the tattered screen in the Palace Cinema, Knottingley, by the OLD MAN, *who coughs and laughs and makes triumphant whoops as he watches the Allied damage of Dresden as he might have done at the newsreel in that cinema fifty years before.*

47

Then the OLD MAN *becomes silent, concentrating and inhaling cigarette smoke deeply. A recognition of the fifty intervening years sobers the* OLD MAN'*s impersonation of his younger self. He is overcome with sobbing. He coughs. He lights another cigarette.*

The image of the tattered screen becomes a still again, displayed in the hands of one of the THREE BOYS *standing beneath Prometheus, and we widen out back in the stadium in Dresden, with* HERMES *conducting the gathered ghosts with his caduceus.*

118. EXT. FOOTBALL STADIUM, DRESDEN, NIGHT

CHORUS OF GHOSTS
Kirchen und Kapellen,
Funfundzwanzig zerstort.

Sehenwurdigkeiten,
Siebzehn zerstort.

Theater und Oper,
Alle funf zerstsort.

Waren und Kaufhauser,
Einunddreissig zerstort.

Hotels und Gastatten,
Siebenundfunfzig zerstort.

Bankhauser,
Vierundzwanzig zerstort.

Lichtspielhauser,
Neunzehn zerstort.

Total Gebaude,
Elftausendneunhundertundsechzehen zerstort.

Total Manner, Frauen und Kinder,
Funfunddreissigtausend zerstort.

HERMES *acts as the conductor of the anti-Promethean* CHORUS. *As the* CHORUS *reaches a climax a helicopter shot reveals the* STATUE OF PROMETHEUS *alone in the stadium. The interrogation lights switch off.*

119. EXT. FOOTBALL STADIUM, DRESDEN, NIGHT

The Zeus-eye (helicopter) shot of the 'trial' of Prometheus. The golden statue becomes smaller and smaller.
Then the floodlights switch off: BLACK.

120. EXT. GERMAN/CZECH BORDER, DAY

A Vietnamese sells garden gnomes at a border stop. Prostitutes flag down cars and trucks.

HERMES
> KRATOS and BIA
> like to cross the border here.
> For 50 Marks they get a shag
> or blow-job from some border slag,
> and buy a dwarf from this collection,
> preferably one with an erection.
> A man drives from Dresden in his new
> 'free market' BMW,
> finds a quiet place and parks
> and gets sucked off for 50 Marks.
> Old East-bloc men can now afford a

PHIL HUNT

49

quick blow-job across the border,
when Deutschmarks fell into their laps
at the Berlin Wall's collapse.
After blow-jobs they buy these
new deities from Vietnamese,
who buy these dwarves from Poles and sell
to New Europe's clientele.
Does Europe now say prayers at night
to a trouser-dropping troglodyte?
The new united Europe's dawn's
heralded by louche leprechauns.
The new rich fill their bijou homes
with prick-proud pixies and lewd gnomes.
These gods with red conks and cocks
replace a Pantheon more orthodox.

121. INT. CHURCH, MOST, CZECH REPUBLIC, DAY

VOICE OF HERMES
Europe's given far holier homes
to equally repulsive gnomes,
and used fire to frighten, with Hell's blaze
wrapping the damned in flame duvets.
And Zeus quite likes Mankind to dwell
on the fires of Holocaust and Hell.

IO (MAM) *hides in the Gothic Church in Most: calm, white and beautiful. The statues of angels and saints in gilded wood make wooing, welcoming gestures to the exhausted woman. One angel serenades her weary spirit with a harp, another with a cello. She feels the temptation of abandon.*
   She sees the friezes of hellfire and its denizens. She gravitates to the candles underneath a crucified Christ.

VOICE OF HERMES
But candles in fire's gentler guise
makes Zeus throw lightning round the skies.
KRATOS and BIA can cut up rough
when they find candlelight to snuff.
And when she closes her cow eyes
feeling safe, Surprise! Surprise!

51

IO *is almost asleep on her feet when she hears the sound of the heavy church door being opened and a pair of rubber boots running towards her. She hurriedly steals a candle and runs along a white colonnade and out of the church, protecting the candle flame with a cupped hand as she runs, desperate to keep it alight to give her the source of a fire in the nights she spends in the open.*

IO *runs and jumps on a Litvinov tram as* KRATOS *and* BIA *pursue her. The candle is still burning in her hand.*

122. INT. TRAM, MOST, CZECH REPUBLIC, DAY
IO *leaps on the tram as it moves off and saves her from her pursuers, but a* MALE PASSENGER *turns on her as she enters and shouts that she mustn't have a lighted candle as the tram goes through potentially dangerous chemical emissions. The whole length of the tramway has signs that reinforce this message. The* MALE PASSENGER *blows out the lighted candle.*

A WOMAN *takes pity on her, realizing that this dirty, ragged woman has no ticket, and punches one of her own tickets and gives it to* IO. IO *sits down and the wax from her extinguished candle runs over her hands.*

The tram passes the chemical works on the right, and on the left IO *sees the truck with the* STATUE OF PROMETHEUS.

123. EXT. TRAM TERMINUS, MOST, CZECH REPUBLIC, DAY
IO *alights and runs with her extinguished candle through a long subway. She runs away at great speed.*

124. INT. PALACE CINEMA, KNOTTINGLEY, DAY
HERMES *is pointing with his caduceus at signs saying, in Czech, 'Switch off engines when red light is flashing' –* Svítí-li červena *– stop –* nékuřte výpněte motory.

HERMES
    Very inflammable. It could go off
    at any moment. Litvinov.

HERMES *reads the warning sign in Czech:*
    Svítí-li červena . . . ńekuřte!
    You, you smoke-wracked wreck
    Nekuřte means Don't Smoke in Czech.
    And you, with the popcorn and the pop,

do you know *Stop* in Czech means *Stop*?
When the warning light here flashes red
tram-drivers brake and quake with dread.
With such combustible emissions
cars have to switch off their ignitions
or everything on track or road
'd automatically explode.
It's so volatile all it 'd need
's some wanker with his fennel weed,
old curdled crud-lung with his brand
of carcinogenous contraband,
to blow the whole caboodle through
all your screens and over you.
Well, let that smoke-wracked scoffer scoff,
he'll croak soon from his smoker's cough
and that collected coal-dust clung
round the crumbling walls of his one lung.
All the smoke's come home to roost
from all the fires his coal produced.

The defiant OLD MAN *raises his Promethean fist and stands.*

OLD MAN
And I were glad we could produce
fuel for fires that angered Zeus.
That bloody Zeus that you kowtow to
but a man like me will never bow to!
Power stations fuelled by t'pits
blow smoke at you immortal shits.

OLD MAN *coughs with the effort of defiance. He collapses into his stalls seat.*

HERMES (*smiling at his predicament*)
It's doomed, all that. You wasted time
grovelling underground in grime.
Those steaming fortresses you pray
'll last till your grandchildren's day
are doomed, *doomed*, on their way out,
destined (as you'd say) to be *nowt*!
Nowt! Nowt! Nowt! Nowt!

55

OLD MAN
    They'll outlast me.
HERMES

                   Without a doubt!
Before this screen here reads THE END
you'll be dead, my croaking friend.
OLD MAN
    Well, I'm not sorry that I'm ailing
    seeing t'dream I worked for failing.
HERMES
    History spat you out like phlegm,
    shop-steward of the NUM
    expecting, of all things, to create
    in class-torn Britain a fair state!
    So I'd unclench your weedy fist
    you smoke-demolished Socialist.
OLD MAN *has a coughing fit.*

125. EXT. WARNING SIGN, LITVINOV, CZECH REPUBLIC, DAY
HERMES *sweeps his caduceus across the screen, which recolours up.*

126. EXT. HERKULES COAL CO, MOST/LITVINOV, CZECH
REPUBLIC, DAY
IO *runs up a path past a sign with the name 'Herkules' written on it.
Hold on sign.*
The STATUE OF PROMETHEUS *continues its journey.*

127. EXT. USTI NAD LABEM, MOST EDVARDA BENEŠE, DAY
*The Statue of Prometheus passes over the Beneš Bridge, and at the same
time the* DAUGHTERS OF OCEAN *pass singing beneath it. They look
towards a derelict hotel on the wooded hillside.*
In the derelict Palace Hotel is IO, *watching.*

128. EXT. DERELICT PALACE HOTEL, USTI NAD LABEM, DAY
IO *runs along a hedge and sees the hotel, and enters by the steps that
lead into the totally derelict foyer.*

129. INT. DERELICT PALACE HOTEL, USTI NAD LABEM, DAY
IO *enters the derelict foyer. The roof of the floor above has collapsed into
the foyer. On one wall are the remains of a painting of a girl in Czech
costume holding a large glass of beer marked '12'. The inscription
beneath the peasant girl is fragmentary but probably reads:* Pivo dobre,
devky hezke/jsou dary země česke.

IO *walks towards the stairs covered with rubble. She has found a haven to rest from running across Europe.*

130. INT. DERELICT PALACE HOTEL, USTI NAD LABEM, DAY
IO *goes into an upstairs room and looks out of the glassless windows. She sees on the Beneš Bridge below the* STATUE OF PROMETHEUS *passing.*

131. INT. KITCHEN OF DERELICT PALACE HOTEL, USTI NAD LABEM, DUSK
IO *lights a fire against the white tiles of the kitchen. She sleeps with firelight dancing on her face.*

A sign forbidding all forms of fire, with icons of the pipe and the candle, with the red slash of the forbidden through them, is above her head. It reads: Zakaz kouřeni a manipulace s ohnem (*Smoking forbidden and all use of fire*).

VOICE OF HERMES
Let the poor cow have her forty winks
though we're much closer than she thinks.
IO (*dreaming*)
Nein.
VOICE OF HERMES
I'll wave my wand and make her dream
of what's deemed Europe's worst regime,
IO (*dreaming*)
Nein.
VOICE OF HERMES
though Zeus approved it and endorsed
the Fuhrer's flames of . . . Holocaust.

Mix through the sign saying 'Zakaz Kouřeni a manipulace s ohnem', with candle and pipe ringed in red, to many Jewish memorial candles in tin holders with Star of David and Yohrzeit (*remembrance*) *inscribed on them.*

132. INT. CREMATORIUM OVENS, AUSCHWITZ, DAY
A JEWISH PILGRIM *places a candle in the dark mouth of a crematorium oven in Auschwitz. He gazes at the candle intently for some time.*

The candle flame and oven are reflected in his glasses.

*He leaves the crematorium, and we find him at the end of the
railtrack that leads through the gateway of Birkenau.*

133. EXT. RAILTRACK, BIRKENAU, DUSK
The JEWISH PILGRIM *places another candle on the rail track.*
*Crane up and reveal the camp and the huts, and the lonely figure
walking down the railtrack, and pick up the* JEWISH PILGRIM *leaving
through the entrance of Birkenau.*

134. EXT. BIRKENAU, DUSK
The JEWISH PILGRIM *leaves through the gateway of Birkenau.*

135. EXT. NEAR AUSCHWITZ, POLAND, NIGHT
The STATUE OF PROMETHEUS *is still, and in its body are reflected
thousands of candles of the sort lit by the* JEWISH PILGRIM.
*Crane down body with hundreds of reflections to CUs of candles
themselves.*
The truck that carries the STATUE OF PROMETHEUS *has its trailer
filled with the little Jewish nightlights we saw in the crematoria and
along the railway lines of Birkenau, and other candles of various kinds.
They burn over the whole surface of the trailer and glow in the golden
body of Prometheus.*

HERMES
   Flames when they are used for light
   most undermine Lord Zeus's might.
   Zeus particularly dislikes
   such stolen fire in little spikes
   like these, fire that renews
   the eagle-ravaged hearts of Jews.
   Why? Why is it fire that they choose?
   These candles that can help them cope
   with history and lack of hope
   are anathema to Fuhrer Zeus
   who hates fire's sacramental use,
   Jews flaunting in Lord Zeus's face
   the fire he'd meant to end their race.

   Zeus and his henchmen have a fit
   whenever they see candles lit.
   The only time they don't is when
   they're in the hands of Zeus's men,
   who happily apply their heat
   to the soles of prisoners' feet.
   Every 'human rights abuse'
   had its proud origin in Zeus,
   who deemed that Man was only fit
   for dumping dead in a mass pit.

HERMES *sweeps away a huge pile of burning Jewish candles.*

   KRATOS! BIA!
   Come and help me over here.

KRATOS *and* BIA *come over and jump on the trailer. They stamp out the nightlights and kick them, some still burning, off the truck.*

136. EXT. NOWA HUTA, POLAND, DAY
Factory chimney in Nowa Huta. The caduceus conducts the camera's movement down from the smoke and down the chimney to the Christ and crucifix outside the steelworks.
   Outside the Bar Meksyk looking at the statue of Jesus on the cross, with a smoking chimney seemingly coming from the crucifix.

HERMES *sitting with a drink in the Bar Meksyk facing a smoking chimney from the industrial complex of Nowa Huta.*

HERMES
  Ognia zlodzeju!

When forms of fire get men destroyed
Zeus is more than overjoyed.
Zeus won't feel properly reimbursed
until Mankind endures the worst.
You'd think that he'd be satisfied
with Europe's toll of genocide.
But when he hears the children wheeze,
those brought up near plants like these,
Zeus now thinks if he bides his time
that though Prometheus and his crime
get flaunted here, that restitution
could take the form of air pollution,
children coughing, little tots
with nebulizers in their cots,
cancer and asthma, if we wait,
might, thinks Zeus, part compensate.
And save him from doing something rash
like end Earth with one lightning flash.
He prefers men die from their own use
of what Prometheus stole from Zeus.
It's long been Zeus's fervent hope
by giving men sufficient rope
and simply allowing a free hand
with stolen fire, the contraband,
that fire will blow up in the face
of the whole detested human race.
The big blow up! Or bit by bit
sink Man slowly in the shit,
the slower but secure solution,
poisoned by his own pollution.
Let such factories do their work
and swathe Mankind in acrid murk.

And if not Armageddon dream a
universal emphesyma!

138. INT. PALACE CINEMA, DAY
OLD MAN *wheezing.* HERMES *delighted at the sound of coughing and
rattling phlegm.*

139. INT. BAR MEKSYK, POLAND, DAY

HERMES
So such Promethean shrines,
chemical and steel works, mines,
still anger Zeus because they stand
for the Promethean contraband,
nonetheless make him content
by blighting Man's environment.

HERMES *looks at the two remaining vodkas on the table.*

I'll drink Kratos's and Bia's!
Not nectar, but who cares. Cheers!

HERMES *knocks back one of the glasses. He is about to do the same with
the second when he hears then sees the* STATUE OF PROMETHEUS *being*

PHIL HUNT

overtaken by two fire-engines, their lights flashing and the BOY*'s distant voice as its wailing siren.*

HERMES *rises and leaves the Bar Meksyk.*

140. EXT. STEELWORKS, NOWA HUTA, DAY

HERMES
And now I intend to introduce
the workers to this foe of Zeus,
and hope their fierce opprobrium falls
on falsely glittering Goldenballs!

HERMES *enters the steelworks.*

141. INT. STEELWORKS, NOWA HUTA, DAY
STEELWORKERS *tending vats of molten metal. Smoke and orange light.*
The STATUE OF PROMETHEUS *enters the furnace room, with shafts of sunlight slanting through the smoke and glowing cauldrons and showers of sparks.*
The scene becomes black and white, like a propaganda film for heroes of Soviet labour.

142. INT. PALACE CINEMA, KNOTTINGLEY, DAY
The picture is revealed as being on the tattered screen of the Palace Cinema, Knottingley. The OLD MAN *shouts out to the Polish* STEELWORKERS.

OLD MAN
Raise your clenched fists to show you praise
t' founder of your foundry's blaze!

Gradually the STEELWORKERS *surround the Statue and, as one man, raise their fists in the Promethean pose.*
Their image changes from black and white to colour.
This is not what HERMES *intended. He is furious. He runs round the ring of* STEELWORKERS *shouting* 'ognia zlodzeju!' (*Thief of Fire!*), *but the* WORKERS *are merely further stimulated into chanting the name of Prometheus, and making the Promethean fist.*

WORKERS
Prometeusz! Prometeusz! Prometeusz!

The OLD MAN *is overjoyed at their response. He feels the old 'solidarity'.*

143. EXT. STEELWORKS, NOWA HUTA, POLAND, DAY

HERMES
    I should have known these stubborn Poles
    still had Prometheus in their souls.
    It angers Zeus. It riles. It galls
    such grovelling to Goldenballs.

    (*to* KRATOS *and* BIA)
    KRATOS! BIA! Get Prometheus out of here!

144. EXT. NOWA HUTA, STEELWORKS, DAY
The golden STATUE OF PROMETHEUS *passes the broken windows of
the steelworks, and is reflected in grimy pools with green hydrants.*

VOICE OF HERMES
    We'll find another place and time
    to bespatter Goldenballs with grime.
    Leave these Poles their smog and smoke
    and may their little children choke,
    and croak inside a plastic bubble
    and save man-hating Zeus the trouble!

145. EXT. STATUE OF HEROIC WORKER, POLAND, DAY
The STATUE OF PROMETHEUS *passes by the statue of a heroic worker
with red flag on the wall of a building near the steelworks.*

146. EXT. BACKYARD NEAR ROADSIDE, POLAND, DAY
IO *runs in and snatches a shirt from a washing line.*
    *She runs through long grass. She reaches roadside and runs past
trucks and a haycart drawn by horses.*

147. EXT. BAROQUE STREETS, BRATISLAVA, NIGHT
IO *rummages in dustbins and gobbles down the fish-heads she finds
there. She washes them down by sucking the dregs of a discarded packet
of 'Zeus juice'.*

148. EXT. BRATISLAVA BRIDGE, SLOVAK REPUBLIC, DAWN
The STATUE OF PROMETHEUS *passes over the bridge. The*
DAUGHTERS OF OCEAN *pass under the bridge, singing.*

149. EXT. GIANT EAGLE MONUMENT, TATABANYA, HUNGARY, DAY

HERMES *beside the eagle of Tatabanya (the 'Turul' monument).*

HERMES *POV of the* STATUE OF PROMETHEUS *being overtaken on the road below by a Tatabanya fire-engine with its lights flashing and its sirens wailing (*BOY *in wreckers' yard making fire-engine noises).*

HERMES

This is the eagle always sent
to deal out Zeus's punishment,
the one whose darkening wingspan soars
over Europe's past and recent wars,
whose shadow bulks large in the sky
when nations are about to die.
This is Zeus's favourite pet
and he hasn't finished eating yet!
He exists to make Man's spirit quake
and in the end to make it break.
The eagle's only got to fly
above a town to terrify,

and has flown more than one mission
after the Yugoslav partition,
urging Serb and Croat side
into committing genocide.
He didn't care which side killed which,
the Serbs of Slobodan Milosevic
or Muslims, it didn't matter who
so long as the death-tolls grew and grew.

Fire-engine overtakes the STATUE OF PROMETHEUS.

And soon the eagle's cruel beak
'll make Prometheus scream in Greek,
and shriek αιαι αιαι αιαι
to the Elefsina sky,
where burn-off flame and petrol fume
will witness the fire-thief's cruel doom.

On the road below we see the STATUE OF PROMETHEUS *about to pass*
beneath the eagle. It is suddenly overtaken by a Tatabanya fire-engine
with its lights flashing and the distant voice of the BOY *as its wailing*
siren.

NICK WALL

150. EXT. WRECKING YARD, DAY
The sound of the BOY *mixes through fire-engine sirens. We see him still driving his wrecked fire-engine in the wreckers' yard.*

151. EXT. BAILE HERCULANE, ROMANIA, DAY
The STATUE OF PROMETHEUS *passes the statue of Hercules in the square of Baile Herculane.*

152. EXT. RAILWAY STATION, BAILE HERCULANE, ROMANIA, DAY
IO *looks at the train time-table, desperately weary. She rests her head against the glass door leading to the platform. The glass door is engraved with the figure of Hercules. She drops off into sleep, then suddenly runs to jump onto the departing train.*

153. INT. ROMANIAN RAILWAY TRAIN, DAY
IO *finds a seat on the train. The other passengers stare at her.*
   IO *sees the* STATUE OF PROMETHEUS *from the train.*
   The TICKET COLLECTOR *begins inspecting tickets. He shouts at* IO, *then throws her off the train, shouting obscenities after her.*

154. EXT. GYPSY VILLAGE, ROMANIA, DAY
IO *walks towards the gypsy village, hoping to be taken in. The villagers look at her suspiciously, then begin to chase her and throw stones at her.* IO *flees.*

155. EXT. MONASTERY, ROMANIA, DAY
A monk in black robes beats a tuaca, *a long plank carried over the shoulder and beaten with a wooden mallet.*
   Outside a small building there are metal receptacles for votive candles for the living and the dead. To the sound of the tuaca IO *enters the building and steals a candle from the many burning there.*
   IO *runs away with the candle.*
   The monk now beats a much bigger tuaca *suspended from chains.*

156. EXT. FIRE STATION, ROMANIA, DAY
The STATUE OF PROMETHEUS *passes an old fire-engine with flat tyres. We hear the* BOY's *siren sound running down, then a cough.*

157. EXT. FOREST, ROMANIA, DAY
The STATUE OF PROMETHEUS *passes a sign warning of the dangers of fire.*
   The caduceus of HERMES *points to the word* FOC *(Fire).*

NICK WALL

158. EXT. VAST DAM, ROMANIA, DAY
The STATUE OF PROMETHEUS *crosses a vast dam.*

159. EXT. DERELICT CARBON FACTORY, COPŞA MICĂ, ROMANIA, DAY
HERMES *on a high vantage point of the derelict carbon works.*

HERMES
    This dereliction, and these hills
    I'll blizzard now with dollar bills.
    Each dollar buys a missile hurled
    at the champion of the human world
    by these jobless carbon worker sods
    who take his side against us gods.
    Or *did* with due devotion till
    they deified the dollar bill.
    Zeus entrusts these jobs to me,
    free-trade Hermes/Mercury!
    When jobs collapse they know their pal
    is *D-mark*-toting Capital!
    One they worshipped not far back
    they now bombard with carbon black.
    How were they converted to bombard
    one they'd worshipped? It's not hard!
    Hard currency is all I need,
    some greenbacks and their human greed.
    Lire or a bit of sterling
    'll soon get these guys missile hurling.

    Do your former worshippers frighten
    the rebel-fisted golden Titan?
    Isn't it frightening a few notes
    can make Prometheans turn their coats?
    For a few dollars they'll shout abuse
    that gladdens the god's ears of Zeus.
    And that's especially because
    here, if anywhere, Prometheus *was*
    patron saint of Copşa Mică,
    industrial Utopia seeker,
    the power to the people fist

71

made him the gilded Socialist.
Now look at all these 'socialists'
with dollar bills in their clenched fists.

HERMES *drops dollar bills from the tower. The Copşa Mică Carbon*
Workers scrabble for them and brandish their dollars.
The CARBON WORKERS *throw carbon at the* STATUE OF
PROMETHEUS.
The scenes changes from colour to black and white. The scene is
projected on the tattered screen of the Palace Cinema.

160. INT. PALACE CINEMA, DAY
The OLD MAN *is on his feet pleading the Romanian* CARBON WORKERS.

OLD MAN
    Don't chuck it! Don't! Don't chuck muck
    at Prometheus. It'll bring bad luck.
    You're desecrating the ideal
    of industry, coal, iron, steel
    and whatever muck that you produce
    or used to till bought off by Zeus.
HERMES *(from screen)*
    Do behave! There's a good chap!
    Applaud these deeds or have a nap
    Or watch, in Socialism's heart,
    how free-trade makes them fall apart.
    I'm winning here. So either clap
    these carbon-chuckers or 'shut thi trap.'
OLD MAN
    Don't, brothers! Stop! All t'old bosses
    'll cash in quick on t'workers' losses.
    The 'free' market'll just leave you broke.
    All our livings have gone up in smoke
    or demolition dust-clouds.
HERMES
                        Just like you.
    Your own demolition 's almost due!

The clouds of carbon thrown by the CARBON WORKERS *make the* OLD
MAN *cough and sit down. He stares in despair at the scene, and closes*
his eyes with horror.

OLD MAN (*to himself*)
 Spatter Prometheus now wi' shit
 but you're t'real targets getting hit.
 He's tricking you, the bastard. Look
 how you're muckied by t'stuff you chuck.
 You cake Prometheus with chucked crud
 and end, as Hermes knew you would,
 with just as thick a coat of black
 as t'god he bribed you to attack.
 You think it's Prometheus you defile
 by smearing him, and all the while
 Hermes knows (that's why he's smiling!)
 it's you yersens that you're defiling.
 That's why that silver sod there's sneering,
 it's your own souls this carbon's smearing.
 He's killing two birds with one stone,
 the spirit of Prometheus, and your own.

The OLD MAN *bursts into a fit of coughing as a cloud of carbon envelops him.*

The CARBON WORKERS *bombard the* STATUE OF PROMETHEUS *with carbon black. The image turns back to colour.*

The STATUE OF PROMETHEUS *is black with carbon.*

IO *comes to the statue and tries to wash it clean. She wipes the feet clean with her hair. She rips off her ragged skirt and uses it to clean off the carbon. She begins to kiss the statue's calf and foot.*

Rain begins washing off the carbon. Thunder rolls through the derelict plant.

CUs of carbon streaming off the gold in rivulets of rain.

161. EXT. DERELICT CARBON FACTORY, DAY
The truck carrying the Statue of Prometheus leaves the derelict factory with rain lashing down. CU of rain on water.

162. EXT. IRON GATES, ROMANIA, DAY
The STATUE OF PROMETHEUS *comes down the road parallel to the Danube flowing into the locks of Portile de Fier (Iron Gates).*

The DAUGHTERS OF OCEAN *pass through the lock, singing.*

VOICE OF HERMES
 KRATOS (Force) and (Violence) BIA,

73

NICK WALL

74

who miss their old SS career,
had recent sport in two regimes
on either side these Danube's streams.
Where our sugary chorus glide
through killing fields on either side,
BIA (Violence) and KRATOS (Force)
found two dictators to endorse,
the best they'd had since World War II,
Milosevic and Ceausescu,
who made the Danube red not blue.
And poor mortals think that song redeems
the ravages of such regimes.

163. EXT. SUNFLOWER FIELDS AND BEE-HIVES, ROMANIA, DAY
The STATUE OF PROMETHEUS *passes vast fields of sunflowers, where*
TWO BEEKEEPERS *watch it go by. Hives are loaded on a truck and
driven into the fields.*

164. EXT. STEELWORKS, BULGARIA, DAY
A rainbow arcs above a run-down steelworks.

VOICE OF HERMES
Look how the free-trade rainbow arcs
in the hues of dollars, sterling, Marks,
but what they'll find at the end of it
's not gold, but a crock of shit.

The silver STATUE OF HERMES *points towards the hoarding
surrounding Kremikovits Steelworks.*

HERMES (*pointing his caduceus*)
Though this is a Promethean shrine
the image painted there is mine.
The image of Hermes painted on a
Bulgarian steelworks. What an honour!
And with a *dogofor* (contract!) in my hand,
doing deals from land to land.
I do hope you don't mind if I gloss
such foreign words we come across,
I hate to flaunt my language skill,
and wouldn't have to, if yours weren't nil!

75

The god of free trade to be hailed,
now that Socialism's failed.
As god of free trade I endorse
the factory's new free-trade course.
Once they aimed at work for all,
now the weak go to the wall.

As HERMES *speaks his image with the steelworks chimneys behind turns black and white, and then appears tattered on the fragmentary screen at the Palace Cinema, Knottingley, where the* OLD MAN *is listening and smoking. The transition is worked through the smoking chimneys to the smoky cinema and smoking cigarette.*

165. INT. PALACE CINEMA, DAY

OLD MAN
But I know that it'll come,
the new Socialist millennium.

HERMES
You must be joking!
Your brain's been addled by your smoking.
You yourself are one of the weak
gone to the wall whereof I speak.
Your suicide by cigarettes
is not a fate that Zeus regrets.
And the free trade I promote
's to help Mankind cut its own throat.

OLD MAN
It's just as well I'll pop mi clogs
when Socialism's gone to t'dogs.
It'd be a struggle to exist
in t'world and *not* be socialist.
How could I go on existing
wi' t'war still on wi'out enlisting?
When men see all they knew collapse
t'old gods start to bait their traps.
Why else is Hermes on the loose
touting for that tyrant Zeus?
When men's great dreams are unemployed
divinities'll fill t'dark void,

76

distributing a specious dole
for every desperate, hungry soul.
I don't need gods, but what I need
's 1. mi Socialism, 2. mi weed.

Though it's med me think I'm allus right
and see t'whole world in black and white,
when life's so infinitely fuller
watched end to end in technicolour.
Wanting t'world all cut and dried
's a form of mental suicide.
And if you asked me now I'd say
that t'world were mostly shades of grey
coloured by a few bright flecks,
like fleeting confetti, love and sex,
and, though I know I'm bloody croaking,
the lifelong joy I've had from smoking.

OLD MAN *exhales a savoured stream of smoke.*

166. INT. BAKERY, JAMBOL, BULGARIA, DAY
A burst of fire from a large paraffin blowtorch into an oven: a WOMAN
heats a small oven with a blowtorch.
   The metal of the bread trays waiting to be baked reflects the fire.
   When the oven is heated enough the WOMAN *withdraws the torch,
puts in the trays of bread and closes the iron shutter to the oven.*

167. EXT. BAKERY, JAMBOL, BULGARIA, DAY
IO, *drawn by the smell of baking bread, approaches the doorway of the
bakery where the* WOMAN *and her son are baking the morning's bread.*

168. INT. BAKERY, JAMBOL, BULGARIA, DAY
The WOMAN *takes bread out of oven and notices* IO *looking into the
bakery. The* WOMAN *takes pity on her, speaks kindly to her and gives
her a warm loaf, which* IO *clutches to her heart.* IO *walks away.*

169. EXT. TENEMENTS, SANDANSKI, BULGARIA, DAY
IO *walks, clutching the still uneaten loaf of bread given her by the kind
baker woman. Two pairs of rubber-gloved hands seize her arms, the
bread falls to the ground.* IO *struggles free and runs through the blocks of
flats, under a concrete arch and into a chemical works.*
   CU of boot trampling the fallen bread as KRATOS *and* BIA *pursue* IO.

NICK WALL

170. EXT. CHEMICAL WORKS, BULGARIA, DAY

IO *runs along a railway track that runs beside a loading bay for sacks of chemicals. White heaps of chemicals lie on the platform of the loading bay. As she runs* KRATOS *kicks a cloud of white chemicals into her face. She gags and chokes and falls to the ground. She is seized by* KRATOS *and* BIA *and dragged towards the parked cattle-truck. She is thrown inside and driven off past Bulgarian chemical signs and the arch of the factory saying* Neochim.

She is now half-black from carbon and half-white from chemicals, so that she has the brindled appearance of a Friesian cow.

171. INT. CATTLE-TRUCK, BULGARIA, DUSK

IO *is captured solo inside the cattle-truck heading for an abattoir.*

She flings herself against the slats of the truck. She howls. She almost moos like a cow.

Her left hand with the wedding ring bashes rhythmically on the truck slats.

VOICE OF HERMES
    Now I think the time is right,

78

daubed as she is in black and white,
caked with chemicals and carbon. Now
stoke the furnace for our Friesian cow.

172. EXT. ABATTOIR, BULGARIA, DAY
The truck pulls up at an abattoir. IO *is goaded out of her truck.*
  KRATOS *and* BIA *goad* IO *with their own version of the caduceus of
Hermes, which they employ like an electric cattle-prod.*

173. INT. ABATTOIR, BULGARIA, DAY
*The cattle go into the run towards the stun gun one by one. We see them
from behind.*
  *Two Friesian cows are stunned in turn and their carcasses fall out of
the chamber onto a metal grid. They are hooked and hoisted up into the
air on a chain. Their hooves rattle across the metal grid as they are
dragged. More cattle move towards the stunning chamber.*
  *The 'guillotine' doors go up and down, with echoing sonorous clangs.
The colours of rust and metal and brick are close to those of Auschwitz.*
  Then IO *is stunned and falls from the chamber onto the metal grid.*
  *Her head bangs across the bars of the metal grid as she is dragged by
the chain and is hoisted up into the air.*
  The pitched hum of the hoist is almost like that of a cello. IO*'s cello.*
  *CU of head dragging across metal grid. Her face is black and white.
On her white cheek there are three drops of blood like a Pierrot's tears.*
  *The yellow plastic starter button for the carcass hoist swings to and fro
across a white immaculate tiled wall. A blue* Insect-o-cutor *bar is
reflected in the white tiles.*

174. INT. CATTLE BURNING PLACE, BULGARIA, DAY
CU of blue Insect-o-cutor *bars with flies being electrocuted making the
sound now revealed as that of the* caduceus of HERMES.
  Pan up from Insect-o-cutor *to* HERMES: *he is watching the killing
from an observation window, and smiles.*

175. EXT. CATTLE-BURNING PLACE, DAY
*Carcasses are scooped up and incinerated in an oven not unlike that of
Auschwitz. The carcasses burn and disintegrate.*
  Then the scoop picks up IO*'s carcass and feeds it into the oven. The
door is sealed.*
  The caduceus of HERMES *stirs the ashes of cremated cows and
discovers the ring of Io.*

176. EXT. BULGARIAN ROAD THROUGH FIR FOREST, DAY
HERMES *stands before a sign warning of the dangers of fire in the forest in Bulgarian. The caduceus points to the Bulgarian word for fire:*
POZHAR.

HERMES
Kaputted in the abattoir,
the cow's cremated in *pozhar*.
Pozhar, the fire that in a flash
turns fine fir forests into ash.

177. INT. PALACE CINEMA, DAY

HERMES (*on screen*)

And you, you old chain-smoking shit
can get such conflagrations lit.

The OLD MAN *makes a defiant gesture at the screen with his cigarette. The voice of the* BOY *imitating a fire-engine siren.*

178. EXT. GREEK FIRE HAZARD SIGN, ROADSIDE, DAY
The caduceus of HERMES *sweeps down from the depicted flames to the cigarette at the bottom of the roadside sign.*

HERMES
They leave their foul fire-blackened trails,
old codgers with their coffin nails.

179. EXT. STATUE OF AESCHYLUS, ELEFSINA, DAY
HERMES *stands beside the* STATUE OF AESCHYLUS *in Elefsina. He watches the disappearing Statue of Prometheus.*

HERMES
There's one bastard passing by
to end up being chained on high,
so that the world can come to mock
Goldenballs chained to the rock,
helpless, hopeless, heaped with scorn,
here, where Aeschylus was born,
the other bastard (maybe worse!)
who hymned Prometheus in his verse.

180. EXT. MUSEUM TERRACE, ANCIENT SITE, ELEUSIS

HERMES *walks from the Statue of Aeschylus to the ancient site of Eleusis.*

HERMES
But if Aeschylus had lived today
he'd have to write a different play.
He'd change his verses once he'd seen a
burn-off flame at Elefsina,
the chimneys pouring smoke above
the ancient site he used to love,
the chimneys painted red and white
that loom above this sacred site,
and how the sacred torch became
a very different form of flame,
from the initiate's pure torch
to factory fires that scar and scorch,
the corrosive, caustic clouds that eat
the marble of Demeter's wheat,

The caduceus points to a fragment of sculpture showing ears of wheat.

those clouds of chemicals that gnaw
the ancient words we stand before.

HERMES *sweeps his caduceus over the inscription* ΑΓΑΘΗ ΤΥΧΗ.

HERMES
ΑΓΑΘΗ ΤΥΧΗ!
                    I'll translate –
Good luck! Not the fire-thief's fate!
And the end that Man'll come to's sticky
and shortish on ΑΓΑΘΗ ΤΥΧΗ!
Not the sort of words you'd find
wished by Zeus on poor mankind.
Zeus won't shed a single tear
to see Man's good luck disappear.
It would have long since disappeared
if Prometheus hadn't interfered.

181. EXT. ELEUSIS (ELEFSINA), DAY

HERMES *points out the* STATUE OF PROMETHEUS *chained to the rock.*

HERMES

> And there Man's benefactor hangs,
> wracked by regrets and conscience pangs.
> We need no eagle now to gnaw
> when conscience can consume him more.
> More rending than the eagle's beak are
> Dresden, Auschwitz, Copşa Mică.
> He'll have to brood there on his rock
> on fire and *Feuer*, *Pozhar*, *Foc*,
> fire that poisons and pollutes

HERMES *looks down at his feet and sees that he is standing in a pool of petrol.*

> and smears petrol on one's silver boots!
> I'll need the spring of Hippocrene
> to cleanse my boots of gasoline,
> I'll quit this globe Man's made so cruddy
> and leave you with my understudy.

HERMES *turns into his statue.*

182. EXT. ELEFSINA MOUNTAINS, NIGHT
The sun begins to set.

183. INT. PALACE CINEMA, DAY
The OLD MAN *coughs with the eagle of Zeus on the screen before him. The sun is setting in black and white.*

184. EXT. TATABANYA EAGLE, NIGHT
The sun sets behind the eagle of Zeus.

185. EXT. ELEUSIS (ELEFSINA), NIGHT

OLD MAN

> You just get t'first drag down your throat 'n
> some bugger's barking it's *verboten*.

Figures of MINERS *emerge from the rocky surroundings. They have pit helmets with their lights switched on and also more ancient torches of flame.*

> Dictators, deities, they're all t'same
> forbidding men fags, fruit or flame.

First Zeus wi' fire then t'God of t'chapel's
obsession wi' forbidding apples.
One crunch into that contraband
gave men t'knowledge God had banned.
We've got t'knowledge, we've got t'fire,
we've raised ussens up out of t'mire.
Diso-bloody-bedience got us over
t'barbed wire fences of Jehovah.
But men thesens bring back t'barbed wire
round t'Bramleys and round t'bakehouse fire.
There's not one joy but what some berk'll
want it ringed wi a red circle.
Gods or men who're summat similar,
'ermes or some Town Hall 'immler,
those in power'd like t'red ring
round almost bloody everything.

186. EXT. ELEUSIS (ELEFSINA), NIGHT

The audience of MINERS *listens to the speech of the* OLD MAN, *who has become* PROMETHEUS. *Their faces are lit by the torches they carry.*

OLD MAN

Fire, that's brought Man close to t'brink
were t'first to help him dream and think.
Imagine men first freed from t'night
first sitting round t'warm firelight,
safe from t'beasts they allus feared
until Prometheus first appeared.
Watching logs burn, watching coal
created what's been called Man's soul,
that like a . . . (*he coughs*) . . . lung or liver gnawed
at t'orders of t'great overlord,
reasserts, gets rent, and reasserts,
for all its rending and raw hurts,
its fiery nature and its light,
its first defiance of dark night.

OLD MAN *lights a cigarette to the strains of an heroic fanfare. He exhales after a deep drag. As he blows out the smoke we cut to the face*

83

of the golden STATUE OF PROMETHEUS, *who appears to be blowing out the last puff of the* OLD MAN's *inhaled smoke.*

> Fire and poetry, two great powers
> that mek the so-called gods' world OURS!

The audience of MINERS *roar approval and rise to their feet and come forward to the spot beneath where the golden* STATUE OF PROMETHEUS *is chained to the rock.*

MINERS (*shouting*)
> Prometheas! Prometheas!

The chant of the MINERS *fades back into the rock of Eleusis and dies away slowly.*

VOICE OF HERMES (*from statue reflected in pool of gasoline*)
> Beware out there this gasoline
> doesn't seep out through the screen.
> Or else your audience participation
> might consist of your cremation.

187. INT. PALACE CINEMA, DAY
The OLD MAN *sees his opportunity.*

OLD MAN (*holding up smoking cigarette*)
> Mi soggy-ended cigarette'll
> mek bloody Hermes molten metal.
> This half-smoked ciggy that I'll chuck'll
> soon mek bastard's buttocks buckle.
> He's stood in t'petrol and my hand
> 's holding t'lit Promethean brand
> and if them boundaries don't exist
> one flick of this arthritic wrist
> 'll mek that servile silver wet
> sizzle with this cigarette!
> I commit you, Hermes, in the name
> of Prometheus to the power of flame.

OLD MAN *flicks his lighted cigarette stub into the pool of petrol on the screen in the Palace Cinema. The petrol ignites with a great roar and consumes the* STATUE OF HERMES, *which screams like a man on fire.*
OLD MAN *rises in revolutionary triumph over the burning* HERMES.

He puts another cigarette in his mouth then his triumphant expression fades from his face as he sees the fire spread to the DAUGHTERS OF OCEAN, who go on singing higher and higher until their song turns into hideous screaming.

The fire spreads to the mountain and the chained PROMETHEUS, and again we hear the MINERS screaming in the fire of the furnace that melted them down.

The OLD MAN's cigarette drops from his mouth as he slumps back into his seat.

The conflagration continues until the statues representing both the DAUGHTERS OF OCEAN and PROMETHEUS are totally consumed, except for the right fist of PROMETHEUS still chained to the rock.

As the cinema screen itself burns the OLD MAN dies.

188. EXT. ELEUSIS (ELEFSINA), NIGHT
In the pool of the melted HERMES we hear the voice of the god. All that remains is the right hand grasping the caduceus, the god still grimly holding on to power.

VOICE OF HERMES *(from puddle: an icy chuckle)*
Yes, they were genuinely mine,
those screams I do hope chilled your spine.
I think you mortals must agree
my screams worked well (if OTT!).
Fittingly frightening but all fake,
gods feel no wound, no pain, no ache.
It's only you ephemeral squirts
who get to feel base human hurts.

He fell for it! It wasn't hard
to pretend that I was off my guard,
to let him think he had me beat
and engineer his own defeat.
And such deceptions dug the pit
of that clapped out Promethean shit.

The cinema is on fire. The OLD MAN is dead. The whole place is going up in flames.

A charred mask of one remaining DAUGHTER OF OCEAN utters a note and a last expiring sigh, which becomes the sound of the BOY making his fire-engine siren noise.

85

189. EXT. PALACE CINEMA, DAY

Outside the smoking Palace Cinema is parked a derelict fire-engine, the one in which the BOY *travelled in his imagination through Europe. The* BOY *is frantically pulling on the useless bell of the fire-engine to raise the alarm.*

The BOY *jumps out of the fire-engine and runs towards the cooling towers, shouting* Mam! Mam!

The residents of nearby houses come out to see what the commotion is.

190. INT. COOLING TOWER, DAY

The BOY *runs through the derelict cooling tower shouting* Mam! Mam! *His voice echoes in the chamber of the cooling tower.*

VOICE OF HERMES

And at his back he'll always hear
the boots of KRATOS and of BIA!

The voice of HERMES *echoes in the cooling towers.*
The cooling towers collapse around the BOY.
He runs through giant dust-clouds.

THE END